D0359356

EXPERIMENTS
---- FOR ----
NEWLYWEDS

50 **AMAZING**
SCIENCE PROJECTS
YOU CAN PERFORM
WITH YOUR SPOUSE

SHAUN GALLAGHER

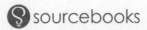
sourcebooks

To Tanya

This publication is designed to provide accurate and authoritative information in regard to the subject matter covered. It is sold with the understanding that the publisher is not engaged in rendering legal, accounting, or other professional service. If legal advice or other expert assistance is required, the services of a competent professional person should be sought.—*From a Declaration of Principles Jointly Adopted by a Committee of the American Bar Association and a Committee of Publishers and Associations*

This book is not intended as a substitute for medical advice from a qualified physician. The intent of this book is to provide accurate general information in regard to the subject matter covered. If medical advice or other expert help is needed, the services of an appropriate medical professional should be sought.

All brand names and product names used in this book are trademarks, registered trademarks, or trade names of their respective holders. Sourcebooks, Inc., is not associated with any product or vendor in this book.

Published by Sourcebooks, Inc.
P.O. Box 4410, Naperville, Illinois 60563-4410
(630) 961-3900
Fax: (630) 961-2168
sourcebooks.com

Library of Congress Cataloging-in-Publication data is on file with the publisher.

Printed and bound in the United States of America.
VP 10 9 8 7 6 5 4 3 2 1

CONTENTS

Try a Challenge

Crunch the Numbers

Write It Out

Check In Over Time

Use Your Senses

Compare Opinions

INTRODUCTION

IF YOU'RE LIKE MANY READERS of this book, you have very recently done the following three things:

- Tied the knot.
- Set off on a romantic honeymoon.
- Discovered a copy of this book tucked in your luggage. (Because what else are newlyweds going to do on their honeymoon besides science experiments?)

If that describes you well, then congratulations, and enjoy your trip!

But maybe that doesn't describe you at all. Maybe you and your significant other are not even engaged, but would like to get to know each other better. Or maybe you are oldy-weds, rather than newlyweds, hoping to spice up your normal routine. Whatever the case, don't let the word "newlyweds" in the title deter you. The experiments can be performed regardless of your marital status or the number of anniversaries you've racked up, and they're all intended to help you learn something new about your partner, strengthen your relationship, and have fun—all in the nerdiest way possible.

Each of the fifty science projects in this book is an adaptation of a real study published in a scientific journal during the past twenty years. The fields of study are varied—psychology, game theory, neuroscience, physiology—but every project can be completed by you and your partner, with no special equipment needed.

Some of the projects are designed to help you understand yourself or your spouse a little better. Others are designed to help you better understand your relationship and the factors that can influence its quality. A handful of the projects were selected not because they reveal any big truths about you or your relationship, but because they're fun for couples to do together. However, even with those projects, you might be able to glean a few marriage-enriching insights along the way.

It's worth pointing out that there are some limitations inherent in adapting published research. For instance, some of the adapted studies recruited research subjects in a narrow age range, such as undergraduate students who participated for course credit. It may be the case that those studies' conclusions are applicable to people of all ages, or it may not. But if you or your partner happen to be outside the age range of the subjects in the source material, don't be afraid to try those experiments anyway. Who knows? You might break new ground!

Similarly, in many of the source studies, particularly those involving romantic couples, only heterosexual couples in long-term relationships are studied. It is entirely possible that the results also apply to relationships outside the demographics of those included in the study, but it is also possible that other types of relationships exhibit different patterns. Again, don't let the limitations of the source material deter you from conducting your own research!

One thing this book does not do is diagnose problems with your marriage. Instead, it's intended to reveal researched-backed insights into what makes healthy relationships work and how to better understand and work with your own feelings and behaviors, as well as your spouse's. It's also intended to help strengthen the bond between you and your partner and give you plenty of fun, slightly geeky activities that you can do in the comfort of your own home.

Enjoy the experiments, and may your marriage be a long and happy one!

HOW TO USE THIS BOOK

For each project, you'll find instructions on how to complete the experiment, a hypothesis predicting a likely outcome, a description of the published research on which the project is based, and practical takeaways to help enhance your relationship.

In many of the projects, one or both of you may be required to read special instructions corresponding to your role in the experiment. These special instructions are tucked away in the back of the book, starting on page 242, and are arranged to minimize the chance that you might peek at your partner's instructions.

If you'd like to approach the projects with scientific rigor, you may want to cover up the hypothesis until you've completed the experiment, so neither of you is unduly influenced.

There is no particular sequence in which the projects need to be completed, so feel free to perform them in whatever order appeals to you. Above all, have fun!

Research Areas:

GET UP AND DO SOMETHING

1
BONDING OVER BONDAGE

 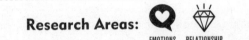
 The experiment

For this experiment, you'll need something to bind your ankles to those of your partner. You can use rope, duct tape, fuzzy handcuffs, or whatever you have on hand.

But before you do that, grab two sheets of paper and separately answer the following four questions about your relationship. For each question, you'll answer on a scale from 1 (lowest possible) to 10 (highest possible):

In general, how satisfied are you with your relationship? _____

How good is your relationship compared to most? _____

To what extent has your relationship met your original

expectations? _____

How well does your partner meet your needs? _____

Now it's time to get to the heart of the experiment: the physical challenge. With your ankles bound together and with each partner holding the other's hands the whole time, your job is to carry a pillow between your bodies from one side of the bedroom to the other, climbing over your bed in the process. You'll need to do this not just once but three times. See if you can complete the task in less than sixty seconds!

Once you've finished and unshackled yourselves, it's time to return to your sheets of paper and separately answer four more questions about your relationship. For each question, answer on a scale from 1 (very infrequently) to 10 (very frequently):

How often do you feel emotionally connected to your
    partner? _____
How often do you get on each other's nerves? ___
How often do you confide in your mate? _____
How often do you laugh together? _____

❓ The hypothesis

You are likely to give your relationship higher marks in the
second set of questions than in the first.

🔬 The research

As part of a 2000 study, couples were asked to complete a relationship satisfaction survey, and then they were randomly assigned to
one of two groups. The first group performed a mundane physical
activity (slowly rolling a ball across the room while on their hands
and knees). The second group performed a task designed to have
several novel elements and to require more physical effort (trans-
porting a pillow across the room while their hands and feet were
bound together, and climbing over a gym mat in the process).
After completing the physical activity, all of the couples then
completed another relationship satisfaction survey.

The researchers found that couples who participated in the novel task showed an increase in relationship satisfaction compared with those who participated in the mundane task, based on comparison of the pre- and post-activity questionnaires.

The fact that an increase in reported relationship satisfaction could be brought about by such an activity surprised the study's authors, who noted that there were strong reasons to expect either no effect (because of the brevity of the activity) or even a negative effect (perhaps brought about by seeing your partner behave awkwardly while trying to shuttle a pillow around the room while bound to you).

Nevertheless, the researchers were pleased that the activity instead led to an increase in relationship satisfaction, because participating in novel, energetic activities is something that most couples can fit into their marriage.

(!) The takeaway

Think back to the first few weeks of your relationship. You likely had frequent, intense conversations, and you might have experienced a level of infatuation that led to physical arousal just by being around the other person. You loved learning new things about them, discovering what you have in common, and the feeling of a deepening relationship. To borrow a term from the study, you were "expanding your selves" by allowing your partner's story to become a part of your story, and there tends to be a positive feeling associated with that expansion.

As newlyweds, you're probably still experiencing a sense of newness and wonder. But as the honeymoon period wears off and you come to know your partner better and better, the opportunities for "expanding your selves" through self-disclosure become less frequent.

Yet as the results of this study reveal, making an effort to experience new things with your partner, particularly those that involve getting your bodies moving, appears to be a way to "expand your selves" anew, or at least to produce the same positive feelings afterward.

So make a plan to regularly try new physical activities, or to put a new spin on some of your old favorites. Book a session at a rock-climbing wall. Play a game of Kabaddi. Or figure out some other novel thing to do with those fuzzy handcuffs.

2
WISHFUL SEEING

Research Areas:

MOTIVATION   PERCEPTION

 The experiment

For this experiment, you'll need a beanbag or some other small object that will not bounce when tossed. You'll also need to agree on a desirable prize, like a restaurant gift card or a TV remote (representing control of the TV for a week), and a prize that's essentially worthless, like a piece of tape or some junk mail. Now, flip a coin to determine who gets to try to win the desirable prize and who gets to try to win the worthless prize.

In separate attempts, place the prize on one side of a large room or hallway and then position yourselves at the other end. Your goal is to toss the beanbag toward the prize. Whoever gets closest to their respective prize is the winner of the game and receives that prize.

Tweak it

Try aiming for the targets again, but this time, try to hit them rather than just come close to them. Do your results change?

The hypothesis

When the goal is to get nearest to the target, the person who is competing for the desirable prize will undershoot the target, while the person who is competing for the worthless prize will not. When the goal is to hit the target, however, neither partner is likely to undershoot.

The research

In multiple studies involving beanbag tossing toward valuable and worthless objects, various researchers observed that the people in the "valuable" condition tend to underthrow compared with people in the "worthless" condition.

In 2009, the authors of one such study came up with an interesting theory about the effect. They suggested that the value of an object influences our perception of how close the object is to us. If that's true, then desirable objects would be perceived as closer than they actually are, which explains the underthrowing.

But that hypothesis was met with some skepticism, and

other researchers set out to come up with alternative explanations for the phenomenon. A 2011 study suggested multiple other reasons for the phenomenon. For example, the people in the "valuable" condition might feel increased pressure to hit the target compared with those in the "worthless" condition, and that might cause them to throw inaccurately. The researchers tested that theory by offering some people a "practice toss" before the real thing, under the assumption that the pressure would be lower during the practice toss. But even in practice tosses, they observed the undershooting.

Another alternate explanation they offered was that the instructions the participants received (the person whose beanbag lands closest to the target wins) might have influenced participants' strategies. They tested that theory by changing the rules. Participants were instructed that they had to actually hit the target to win the prize. Under those modified rules, a pattern of under-tossing was not observed in either the "valuable" or "worthless" condition, which undermined the earlier study's conclusion that valuable objects are perceived as closer than they actually are.

So if it's not the case that people undershoot the target because they perceive it to be closer than it actually is, then what explains the fact that participants in the "valuable" condition undershoot, at least in some circumstances, while those in the "worthless" condition do not? The authors of the 2011 study suggest that people who are trying to win a valuable prize tend to undershoot because they overthink, whereas those who have no particular interest in winning a worthless prize are more likely to behave naturally, and to end up closer to the target as a result.

(‼️) The takeaway

If you're the type of person who can't walk past a carnival booth without trying to win your spouse a giant stuffed teddy bear at the ring toss, now you've learned one of the secrets of high-stakes tossing: don't overthink it. The more strategy you try to use, the less natural your throw is likely to be. The same general principle also holds true in other areas of your married life. Have you ever tried to rehearse a difficult conversation, only to find that when it comes time to actually speak with your spouse, your words come out stilted? Or have you spent time planning a highly structured date night, only to discover that the lack of sponta-neity also dampens the romance? Planning and structure have their place, but by not going overboard, you will allow yourself to act more naturally, and hopefully that will help you hit your target, whatever it may be. And if you fail anyway, don't despair. Maybe your spouse will win the giant stuffed teddy bear for *you*.

3

THE FLOATING ARM TRICK

> **Research Areas:**
>
> MOTOR CONTROL   REFLEXES

 The experiment

In this project, you'll try a little parlor trick that is popular among children and learn a little more about why it works. Select a doorway in your home where you can stand and lift your arms, with the backs of your hands (not your palms) pressing against each side of the doorframe. Take turns standing in this position and pressing firmly against the doorframe, as if you're trying to make it wider, for about a minute. Then step away, put your arms at your sides, and stand still.

The hypothesis

Your arms will slowly "float" upward and may stay raised in that position for several seconds before the effect wears off.

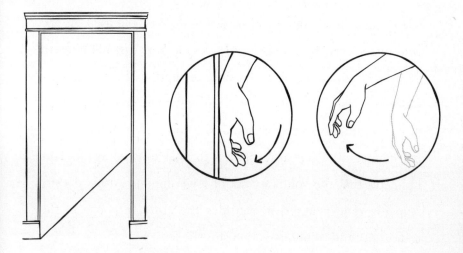

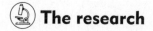 **The research**

This effect is known as Kohnstamm's phenomenon. It's named after German neurologist Oskar Kohnstamm, who first identified it in the early 1900s. After a sustained voluntary contraction of the deltoid muscle, an involuntary contraction occurs, causing the arms to slowly move upward.

Although it may seem like just a fun way to make your husband or wife look silly while standing in a doorway, Kohnstamm's phenomenon has helped researchers better understand how motor control works, and their findings have wide-ranging implications.

For instance, in a 2014 study, researchers monitored the

muscle activity of volunteers as they performed the trick. As the volunteers' arms began to rise, the researchers instructed them to bring their arms back down (interrupting the involuntary movement with a counteracting voluntary movement), which all of the volunteers were able to do. But then something interesting happened. Their arms started to float upward again. This indicates that the voluntary act of lowering one's arms doesn't stop the reflex; rather, it overrides the arms' response to the reflex until the voluntary action stops.

The researchers note that a better understanding of the way involuntary and voluntary actions interact may be useful in treating patients with movement disorders, such as the involuntary tremors associated with Parkinson's disease. It's also a promising line of study for the treatment of tic disorders, such as Tourette's syndrome, because as with Kohnstamm's phenomenon, tics can sometimes be voluntarily suppressed, at least for a short period. Knowing how voluntary and involuntary actions affect and sometimes override each other may lead to new therapies for these disorders.

(!) The takeaway

Who knew a children's parlor trick could teach adults so much about the way our bodies work? Exploring this phenomenon has helped researchers better understand the interplay between voluntary and involuntary movements. Hopefully, testing it out yourselves gives you both an appreciation for not only the strange ways our bodies sometimes operate, but also for the sense of fun and connection you can feel as a couple just by spending time together doing ordinary things. So be on the lookout for other ordinary opportunities: in the kitchen, in the car, or even in the doorway.

4
FEELING SQUEEZED

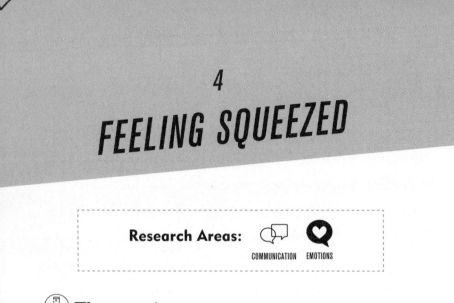

Research Areas: COMMUNICATION EMOTIONS

🧪 The experiment

For this experiment, you'll need a blindfold or eye mask, plus eight slips of paper and a writing instrument. On each slip of paper, write one of the following words:

anger, disgust, fear, happiness, sadness, love, gratitude, sympathy

You and your spouse will be performing an exercise to see if you can communicate certain emotions using only your sense of touch. Flip a coin to decide who will be the Toucher and who will be the Guesser. The Guesser should put the blindfold on and sit with one arm outstretched, so the other spouse can easily touch their forearm.

Toucher, your job is to communicate each of the eight emotions written on the slips of paper to the Guesser. Shuffle the papers, then choose one at a time and try to communicate the emotion by touching your spouse's forearm in whatever way you think appropriately conveys the meaning. After each touch, read the list of eight emotions and ask your partner to guess which one you were trying to communicate.

Tweak it

Repeat the exercise, switching the roles of Toucher and Guesser, but this time don't restrict touches to only the forearm. Rather, touch anywhere on your spouse's body that helps communicate the emotion.

The hypothesis

Your spouse will likely be able to accurately identify anger, fear, disgust, love, gratitude, and sympathy. In the whole-body experiment, your spouse will likely be able to identify happiness and sadness as well.

🔬 The research

In a 2006 study, researchers paired up unacquainted participants and randomly assigned one to the role of Toucher and the other to the role of Guesser. The Toucher's task was to communicate emotions using only touches to the Guesser's forearm. For the emotions of anger, fear, disgust, love, gratitude, and sympathy, more than half of all participants in the Guesser role were able to identify the correct emotion. Happiness and sadness were more difficult; fewer than a third of Guessers identified the correct emotion.

A 2009 study repeated the experiment, but this time the touch could be made anywhere on the Guesser's body, as opposed to just the forearm. With that constraint relaxed, Guessers were able to accurately guess happiness 60 percent of the time and sadness 50 percent of the time.

Researchers in both studies observed that there were well-defined movements and touch patterns associated with the various emotions. For instance, hitting and squeezing conveyed anger; trembling conveyed fear; pushing conveyed disgust; stroking and rubbing conveyed love; shaking conveyed gratitude; and patting conveyed sympathy. In the whole-body experiment, happiness was frequently conveyed by swinging or hugging, and sadness was frequently conveyed with nuzzling or contact that didn't involve movement.

(!) The takeaway

While you're probably pretty attuned to the way your spouse signals emotions using facial and vocal communication, you might have been under the impression that touch plays more of a supporting role, or acts as an intensifier of other verbal or nonverbal communication, rather than a channel of communication in its own right. But the results of this experiment show that a range of emotions can be communicated with reasonable clarity solely through physical contact, even when that contact is constrained to just one part of the body.

Use this knowledge to your advantage. During your marriage, you will likely experience both happy and troubling circumstances as a couple where words fail you. It is during those times when you can let your spouse know how you're feeling through a firm grasp, an excited squeeze, or a gentle caress.

5
TIME WEALTHINESS

Research Areas: PERCEPTION   SOCIAL PSYCHOLOGY

🧪 The experiment

Begin this experiment at the start of your day. Flip a coin to determine which spouse will complete a Self-Focused task and which spouse will complete an Other-Focused task. The spouse assigned to the Self-Focused task should turn to page 242 for further instructions. The spouse assigned to the Other-Focused task should turn to page 252 for further instructions.

After you've both read the instructions for your task, try to complete the task sometime during the day. Then, at the end of the day, once you've both completed your assigned task, reconvene and respond to the following statements, using a scale from 1 (strongly disagree) to 10 (strong agree):

There is plenty of time left in my life to make new
  plans. _____

Most of my life lies ahead of me. _____

As I get older, I begin to experience time as limited. _____

I have the sense that time is running out. _____

🧠 The hypothesis

The spouse who completed the Other-Focused task is likely to have responded with higher values on the first two statements and lower values on the other two statements than the spouse who completed the Self-Focused task.

🔬 The research

In a 2012 study, researchers split participants into two groups. One group was directed to spend time during the day doing something for another person. The other group was directed to spend an equivalent amount of time during the day doing something for themselves. Participants in both groups then answered some questions from the Future Time Perspective scale, developed in a 2002 study to examine people's perspectives on how much time they have available to accomplish their goals. The researchers found that people who spent time doing something for another person reported more "time affluence" (a greater amount of time available to accomplish their goals) than people who spent time on themselves.

In a related experiment, college students were either permitted to leave class fifteen minutes early or asked to remain in class and spend those fifteen minutes helping an at-risk high-school student with an essay. Even though the students who left class early had been given fifteen minutes of unexpected free time, they still later scored lower on the "time affluence" measurements than the students who remained in class to help another person.

ⓘ The takeaway

The results of this research suggest, perhaps counterintuitively, that if you feel as if you don't have enough time in the day to accomplish all of your tasks, one way to change that perception is to give your time to someone else. It appears that sharing your time with others helps you feel more effective overall, and better able to accomplish your own goals. If you or your spouse find yourselves feeling starved for time, it might be worthwhile for you to consider not only penciling in some "me time," or "us time," but also some time spent focused on the needs of others. You can't change the fact that there will always be only twenty-four hours in a day, but you may be able to change how you feel about what you can accomplish in that time.

PART 2

SIT DOWN AND THINK

6
THE MONEY REQUEST GAME

Research Areas:

ECONOMICS   GAME THEORY

The experiment

Imagine that you and your spouse are recruited to play a simple game in which you can earn money. Each of you gets to request an amount of money between $11 and $20. You are each guaranteed to get whichever amount you request. But if your request happens to be $1 less than your partner's, you also earn a $20 bonus.

Each of you should write down the amount of money you wish to request, and then write a brief explanation for your choice. Once you've both made your requests, you can share them with each other and then read on!

❓ The hypothesis

Each of you is very likely to have chosen $17, $18, or $19, and to have explained it methodically, e.g., "My wife probably thinks I'll choose $20, so she'll choose $19, so I'll choose $18." However, if you happen to have chosen an amount lower than $17, you probably did not explain it methodically, but rather as a best guess, without elaborating.

🔬 The research

In one-shot, two-player games like these, not everyone employs the same depth of reasoning. Some people make choices that are nonstrategic; they don't even try to guess what the other person will do, but instead stick to simple rules to make their own choices. In game theory, these choices are called "level-0," because they involve zero beliefs about what the other person might do. Other people use "level-k" strategies (where k is a number greater than 0). For instance, a "level-1" choice assumes the other player's choice will be level-0, a "level-2" choice assumes the other player's choice will be level-1, and so on.

In a 2012 study, two economics professors came up with an exercise that was especially suitable for studying level-k

reasoning. The result was the game you and your spouse just played!

They tested the game on a bunch of economics undergrad students and found that only 6 percent chose $20 (the level-0 choice). The vast majority, 74 percent, chose $17, $18, or $19.

While it's true that every possible choice could be the result of level-k reasoning, when the researchers looked at the students' explanations of their choices, they found that almost without exception, students who chose an amount less than $17 did not do so as a result of level-k reasoning, but generally made a best guess without thinking it through methodically. But nearly everyone who chose $17, $18, or $19 explained their choice methodically, by way of level-k reasoning.

Based on these results, the study's authors concluded that it is relatively rare for people to exercise anything higher than level-3 reasoning (and, in practice, rare that they would need to). As for why that is, they offered no definitive conclusions, but they note that as k grows higher, it becomes more and more difficult for us to hold in our heads all of the information required to make a decision based on those values. So it may be that going beyond level-3 reasoning is just too mentally taxing for the average person, and because our choice hinges on what level of reasoning the other person will use, it's best to not veer too far from average in your prediction.

(!) The takeaway

By now, you and your spouse have shared your results. If your partner underestimated you (say, by requesting $19 when you requested $18), you can at least relish the fact that if you were playing for real money, you would have won the $20 bonus.

You might also want to use these results as a jumping-off point for a conversation about how well (or how poorly) you are able to predict your partner's choices, and about whether that bothers you or excites you. Perhaps you like being able to complete each other's sentences. Or maybe you find it more thrilling that you never quite know what your spouse is going to say next!

THE MAN IN BLACK'S LEVEL-K DUEL

In the film *The Princess Bride*, based on William Goldman's novel of the same name, the mysterious, swashbuckling Man in Black challenges the egomaniacal villain Vizzini to a battle of wits. The Man in Black explains the rules: Into one of two goblets, he has placed deadly poison. All Vizzini needs to do is choose a goblet to drink; the Man in Black will drink the other one, and then one of them will die.

Vizzini, to his credit, recognizes this as a game involving level-k reasoning.

"All I have to do," he announces with bravado, "is divine from what I know of you. Are you the sort of man who would put the poison into his own goblet, or his enemy's? Now, a clever man would put the poison into his own goblet, because he would know that only a great fool would reach for what he was given. I'm not a great fool, so I can clearly not choose the wine in front of you. But you must have known I was not a great fool; you would have counted on it, so I can clearly not choose the wine in front of me!"

The "great fool" he first mentions is a level-0 player: someone who would drink his own goblet without considering his opponent's strategy. His further ruminations go higher up in k values by, for instance, anticipating his opponent's choice based on what he thinks the Man in Black thinks he will choose.

In the end, Vizzini illustrates a key principle about level-k reasoning. It's not the size of your k that earns you the victory. It's whether your opponent's value is k minus 1.

7

CHOOSE YOUR CHOCOLATES

Research Area: CONSUMER PSYCHOLOGY

The experiment

Each of you should read the following two scenarios and separately record your decisions.

Imagine that a local chocolatier has offered you the opportunity to sample some chocolate truffles, and you're permitted to bring along a close friend, such as your maid of honor or best man, to the sampling session. You are asked to select one of two sampling packages. In the first package, you get to sample seven chocolates, and your guest gets to sample three. In the second package, you get to sample two chocolates, and your guest gets to sample four. Your guest will know which of the two packages you've chosen. Which package do you choose?

Next, imagine that instead of having the opportunity

to bring a close friend to the sampling session, you're paired with a casual acquaintance whom you see irregularly. In the presence of that person, you're again given the choice between the same two sampling packages: seven chocolates for you and three for them, or two for you and four for them. Which package do you choose?

ⓟ The hypothesis

You are more likely to choose the first package when your sampling partner is a close friend, but the second package when your sampling partner is a casual acquaintance.

🔬 The research

In a 2015 study, consumer researchers presented a version of the chocolate sampling scenario to participants. Some of the participants were told that their guest would be a close friend, and others were told that their guest would be a casual acquaintance.

The researchers found that participants in the close-friend group chose the first package two-thirds of the time, but those in the casual-acquaintance group chose it only one-third of the time.

The results are in line with what the researchers call a

"friendly taking effect." Basically, the closer your relationship to a person, the more likely you are to view yourself and that person as a collective rather than as separate individuals. Because you're treating the two of you as a collective, you're more likely to base your decision on the total value of a package (ten chocolates total in the first package, versus six in the second), even in cases where the package with the highest total value benefits you more than the other person. Alternatively, they suggest, you might be more likely to choose the first package when a close friend is your guest because you expect them to be more forgiving of what appears to be a selfish choice than a casual acquaintance might be.

(!) The takeaway

It's important for marital harmony to make decisions that affect both of you with a "we" mindset, rather than an "I" mindset. But as this experiment illustrates, sometimes a decision that has the highest total benefit for the two of you ends up benefiting you disproportionately, or it involves passing up on an alternative that might have benefited your spouse slightly more. That can put you into an awkward position, because your spouse might not be very inclined to think in "we" mode when they feel they've been slighted. So talk over these scenarios with your spouse and try to find each other's tolerance for these sorts of imbalanced payoffs. Maybe your spouse wouldn't mind if you selected the first package, because they realize that a gain of a single piece for them would mean a loss of five pieces for you. Or maybe your spouse would feel offended and consider it rude that you would choose a package in which you get more chocolates than your guest. Whatever your spouse's feelings on the matter, it's helpful to know them ahead of time before this scenario plays out in real life. Knowing how your spouse would react can save you from both a headache and a bellyache.

8
BUYING EXPERIENCE

Research Area:

CONSUMER
PSYCHOLOGY

🧪 The experiment

Either together or separately, recall a time when you purchased a material good that cost more than $50 from among a number of different options. (For instance, a new jacket, a couch, or a piece of jewelry.) Next, recall a time when you purchased an experience that cost more than $50 from among a number of different options. (For instance, tickets to a concert, a trip overseas, or dinner at an upscale restaurant.) On a scale from 1 to 10, rank your initial satisfaction with each of the purchases. Then, on the same scale, rank your current satisfaction with the purchases.

❓ The hypothesis

Your initial satisfaction with the two purchases may have been the same, but your satisfaction with the experiential purchase is likely to have endured or even risen over time, whereas your satisfaction with the material purchase is likely to have fallen over time.

🔬 The research

Participants in a 2010 study were asked to recall experiential and material purchases and rate their initial and current satisfaction with those purchases. Although there was no difference in initial satisfaction, participants reported more current satisfaction with their experiential purchases than with their material purchases. In fact, the longer ago the purchase was made, the more divergent the ratings were. Satisfaction with experiential purchases tended to increase over time, whereas satisfaction with material purchases tended to decrease over time.

One of the reasons why this might be so, according to the researchers, is that material goods are easier to compare against each other, making the initial decision more difficult and stressful and leading to enduring comparisons with other goods. A gadget you purchased three years ago might have had similar functionality to similar gadgets at the time of purchase, but now, compared with the latest models, its depreciation and its journey toward obsolescence may be more apparent.

Another reason is that people tend to rationalize bad experiences to a greater degree than they rationalize faulty goods. For instance, if a storm rolls through during a music festival, you might not enjoy getting soaked. However, you might look back later and say, "It was a crazy day, but experiencing it together strengthened our relationship." On the other hand, if your car needs frequent repairs, it's harder to find a silver lining in that.

(!) The takeaway

When deliberating between purchasing a tangible good or an experience, you and your spouse might initially show a preference for the tangible good, reasoning that an experience is fleeting but a tangible good is enduring. The results of this research suggest, however, that the joy we get out of the experience holds up long afterward, but the joy we get out of the tangible good may not. That's true especially when your purchase turns out to be a debacle or a dud. A horrendous honeymoon or a wrong-turn road trip might nevertheless end up being a fond—if slightly embellished—memory between you and your spouse years down the line. Rarely will a too-noisy vacuum cleaner or an itchy sweater do the same.

9
A FOLD LIKE GOLD

Research Areas:

CONSUMER PSYCHOLOGY   ECONOMICS

The experiment

For this experiment, flip a coin to determine which one of you is going to be the Assembler, the one who will perform some paper folding. The Assembler will need a sheet of paper and access to the internet. Use your favorite search engine to find a tutorial on how to fold a paper crane. Follow all of the steps to complete the paper crane, and then show it to your partner.

Now, imagine you'll be selling the paper crane at an upcoming garage sale. You and your spouse should separately decide on a selling price, between 1 cent and 100 cents. You should also privately write down a guess about what price your spouse will set for the creation.

🅟 The hypothesis

The selling price set by the spouse who acted as thc Assembler will be the higher price. Additionally, the Assembler's guess about their spouse's selling price will be higher than the selling price their spouse actually chose.

🔬 The research

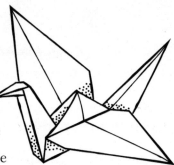

A 2011 study of consumer behavior examined the "IKEA Effect," the idea that we value things more when we assemble them ourselves than when we purchase them preassembled. In a series of experiments, participants assembled furniture items from IKEA, folded paper to create origami, and put together small LEGO sets. They were then given the opportunity to bid for the items they assembled. The study found that they bid significantly more for the items than people who had the opportunity to purchase the same items preassembled. It also found that the assemblers' estimates of what other people would be willing to pay for the items were roughly the same as what they themselves were willing to pay, suggesting that they truly believed their bid was the fair value for the items.

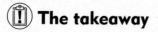 The takeaway

You're newlyweds, so some degree of furniture assembly is likely to be in your immediate future, giving you and your spouse ample opportunities to experience the IKEA Effect. It may help ease some of your frustration, as you labor through the 101-step assembly process and curse the various sizes of hex keys, to know that when the project is complete, your furniture will be imbued not only with strictly utilitarian value, but also with an ineffable value born from the hard work it took to put it all together. Just remember that ten years from now, when you put it out on the lawn during a yard sale, you'll need to subtract that premium from the asking price. Even though you might think it's the most expertly assembled armoire on the resale market, buyers who had no hand in the assembly process might have a more modest opinion.

10
A REMOTE CHANCE

Research Areas: 👓 🧠
CONSTRUAL DECISION
MAKING

🧪 The experiment

Flip a coin to determine who will read the Spouse A Instructions on page 242 and who will read the Spouse B Instructions on page 252. Once you've each read your instructions, return here and evaluate the following options.

The first prize package is a $150 gift card to a bookstore, but the gift card comes with some unique restrictions. It can only be used during the last hour of business each Tuesday, and you can't purchase any books published within the past five years. On a scale from 1 to 10, how interested are you in entering this promotion? Spouse A: _____ Spouse B: _____

The second prize package is a $15 gift card to a bookstore. This gift card does not have any unusual restrictions. It can be used at any time, on any item. On a scale from 1 to 10, how interested are you in entering this promotion? Spouse A: ____ Spouse B: ____

(?) The hypothesis

Spouse A is likely to be more interested in winning the second prize package than the first, whereas Spouse B is likely to be more interested in winning the first prize package than the second.

(🔬) The research

The authors of a 2007 study were curious about whether probability could be thought of as a form of psychological distance, with high-probability events being thought of as "near" and low-probability events being thought of as "far." There are other forms of psychological distance, such as distance in space or time, that can affect how we construe a particular event or situation, and the researchers wanted to test whether probability might work similarly.

They conducted an experiment in which participants were split into four groups. Participants in the first group were presented with a high-value prize that was inconvenient to redeem, and were told that if they opted into the promotion, they were almost certain to win the prize. Participants in the second group were presented with a low-value prize that was easy to redeem, and were again told that if they opted into the promotion, they were almost certain to win the prize. The third and fourth groups were presented with the same prize descriptions; the only difference is that they were told they had only a 1 in 100 chance of winning.

The researchers found that when the probability of winning the prize was low, participants were more interested in the high-value/inconvenient prize than the low-value/convenient prize. But when the probability of winning was high, the preferences were reversed! There was more interest in the low-value/convenient prize than the high-value/inconvenient prize.

These results confirmed the researchers' hypothesis that probability can affect how the prizes are construed. Unlikely outcomes are seen as more distant and are construed at a relatively high level, with participants focusing on the "What" (the value of the prize itself). More likely outcomes appear nearer and are construed at a relatively low level, with participants focusing on the "How" (how easily the prize is redeemed).

(!) The takeaway

One of the benefits of being able to put some mental distance between you and an object of your desire is that it allows you to be more objective in your evaluation and broader in your perspective.

Suppose you and your spouse are considering taking a vacation together. There are various ways in which psychological distance might come into play. There might be temporal distance, if you're planning months ahead. There might be spatial distance, if you're planning to visit an unfamiliar place. And there might be a distance of probability, if the weather is unlikely to cooperate with your outdoor plans or the attractions you wish to visit are unlikely to fit within your budget. This distance can help you better sort your priorities and distinguish between the essentials and the nice-to-haves, leading to a more fulfilling vacation. Or, to put it another way: a big-picture perspective can increase the chance of a picture-perfect getaway.

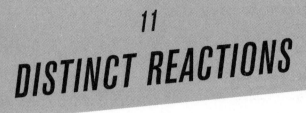

11
DISTINCT REACTIONS

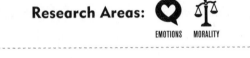

Research Areas: EMOTIONS MORALITY

 The experiment

Each of you should think about a recent time when another person did something immoral and you were the target of their action. It could be something relatively minor, like stealing your parking spot, or something more serious, like stealing your car. Spend a few moments thinking about how the incident made you feel and then rate, on a scale from 1 (very low) to 10 (very high), the degree to which you felt disgust in response to their action. Then rate, on the same scale, the degree to which you felt anger in response to their action.

Next, think about a recent time when another person did something immoral, and you were not the target of their action, but you were present when it happened. Perhaps a friend or a coworker was the target, and you saw the incident unfold. Again, spend a few moments thinking about how the immoral conduct made you feel and rate, on scale from 1 to 10, the degree to which you felt disgust and the degree to which you felt anger in response to their action.

⑦ The hypothesis

In the first scenario, where you were the target of the immoral conduct, you are likely to have experienced more anger than disgust. But in the second scenario, where you witnessed the immoral conduct but were not the target, you are likely to have experienced more disgust than anger.

🔬 The research

Disgust and anger are common and related emotions we experience in response to moral violations. But whether a person reports being disgusted or angry when expressing moral outrage, are they really expressing a single sentiment? Or do the two emotions represent two distinct reactions to immoral behavior?

Researchers in a 2017 study attempted to tease apart the distinction between the two emotional reactions to moral violations. In one experiment, they asked participants to recall

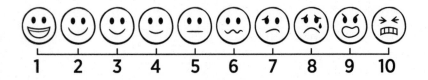

times when they were either the target of a moral violation or a witness to one. The participants rated the degree to which they felt disgusted or angry in response to the incident.

The researchers found that anger was the stronger of the two emotions when the participant was the target, while disgust was the stronger of the two emotions (but just barely) when the participant was a witness.

In a subsequent experiment performed as part of the same study, the researchers found that when anger is the predominant emotion in response to a moral outrage, people are more likely to endorse what might be called "direct aggression," such as physical or verbal confrontation of the perpetrator, and when disgust is the predominant emotion, people are more likely to endorse "indirect aggression," such as social exclusion or attacks on the perpetrator's reputation.

The researchers argue that these results show anger and disgust are two distinct emotional responses to moral outrage. Anger tends to predominate in high-cost situations (when you yourself are the victim), which in turn leads to high-risk responses (such as direct aggression). Disgust, on the other hand, tends to predominate in lower-cost situations (when you are merely a witness), which in turn leads to lower-risk responses (which might not involve confronting the perpetrator directly). Because each emotion is associated with a different response tendency, what each emotion signals to other people might also differ. For instance, an angry response might signal that you're willing to engage in direct aggression if someone offends you, and so it might act as a deterrent toward future offenses. And a disgusted response might signal that you're willing to engage in indirect aggression tactics, which require coordinated social action, so it might act as a way of recruiting others who feel similarly.

(!) The takeaway

The world has no shortage of immorality and an increasingly abundant supply of moral outrage. In fact, between the talking heads on TV and the digital mobs online, you might feel like it's hard to go a day without hearing someone express fury or indignation about someone or something that ticked them off. Depending on your personalities and interests, you and your spouse might also find yourselves in a state of moral outrage, or reacting to others' outrage, and it's helpful to be able to pinpoint exactly what a particular emotional response says about how you view the situation and what you plan to do in response.

The next time you find yourself either the target of or a witness to immoral conduct, talk it over with your spouse. Do your levels of anger or disgust tell you anything about the stakes? Does your visceral response feel like the most prudent way to deal with the situation? Getting in touch with these uncomfortable emotions, and especially doing so with the assistance of your partner, can not only help you better understand yourself but also guide you to make more thoughtful and purposeful decisions about how to address the problem.

12
THE MIND'S EYE

 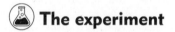
🧪 The experiment

Flip a coin to determine who will be the Experimenter and who will be the Subject. The Subject should answer the following questions on a scale from 1 (no mental image at all) to 10 (clear and as vivid as normal vision):

Think of a friend whom you see regularly, and try to picture their face. How vividly do you see their face in your mind's eye? _____

Think of the last time you saw a spectacular sunrise or sunset. How vividly do you see the colors in your mind's eye? _____

Imagine walking into a familiar store, approaching

the counter, and asking to exchange a dollar bill for four quarters. How vividly does the scene play out in your mind's eye? _____

Next, the Experimenter should follow these instructions to set up the second part of the experiment:

On page 243, you will find three pairs of images. Each image is circular in shape and is made up of parallel black and white bars at a particular angle. Show your spouse the first pair of images, A and B, and ask them to try to remember their orientation. Then turn to page 253 and show them the first test image. Tell your spouse that this image is the same as image B, but it's been turned either 15 degrees clockwise or 15 degrees counterclockwise. Ask your spouse to identify in which direction it was turned, and record the response.

Return to page 243 and show your spouse the second pair of images, C and D, and again ask them to try to remember their orientation. Then turn to page 253 and show them the second test image. Tell your spouse that this image is the same as image C, but it's been turned either 15 degrees clockwise or 15 degrees counterclockwise. Ask your spouse to identify in which direction it was turned, and again record the response.

Finally, return to page 243 and show your spouse the final pair of images, E and F. Then turn to page 253 and show them the third test image. Tell your spouse that this image is the same as image E, but it's been turned either 20 degrees clockwise or 20 degrees counterclockwise. Ask your spouse to identify in which direction it was turned, and again record the response.

❓ The hypothesis

The more vivid your spouse perceives their mental imagery to be, the better they will do at the memory task.

🔬 The research

Scientists use the term "working memory" to refer to short-term memory that is used to hold information for further processing. We use working memory to temporarily hold an unfamiliar phone number in our heads while we dial it, or to store sentence fragments while we translate them from speech to text while taking dictation. One particular type of working memory is visual working memory, in which the information we try to store in memory is visual imagery.

Researchers in a 2011 study wanted to test the link between

the vividness of mental imagery and visual working memory. Their hunch was that people with strong mental imagery would do better on a test of visual working memory than people with poor mental imagery. The researchers first tested the strength of participants' mental imagery. Then, the subjects were given a test of visual working memory similar to the one you performed in your experiment. (For each pair of patterns, both had to be kept in memory until the test image was shown.)

The results of the study showed a positive correlation between strength of mental imagery and the accuracy of visual working memory. Participants who could form clear, vivid mental images in their mind's eye were better able to hold images in their working memory. Fortunately, even participants with poor mental imagery did far better than chance on the visual working memory task, which suggests that they were able to use other nonvisual strategies to keep the information in memory.

The takeaway

It's a decent bet that you and your spouse use your working memory every day, though your accuracy may vary. "Honey, can you pick up milk, eggs, bread, bananas, and dish soap?" might lead to your spouse bringing home the five items you requested, or maybe fewer, or maybe a mix of correct and incorrect items. If you know that you or your spouse struggle with working memory, don't fret. There are a variety of compensatory strategies you can use to make life easier on the both of you. Try employing mnemonics, setting the list of items to music, or offloading the data from your brain to a Post-it Note.

A BLIND MIND'S EYE

It's long been known that people differ in their self-reported ability to conjure up vivid imagery in their mind's eye. Some people report seeing mental images as clearly as they can see with their regular vision, while others appear to experience aphantasia, the utter inability to produce mental imagery.

Although these self-reports, such as those you completed in the experiment, seem reliable, researchers in a 2017 study devised a novel way to objectively measure whether imagery is being conjured in the mind's eye. They made use of a phenomenon called binocular rivalry, where each eye is shown a different pattern, and one of the patterns tends to emerge as the dominant one. A 2008 study had found that priming participants to imagine one of the patterns beforehand strongly influenced whether they would perceive that pattern as the dominant one during the binocular display.

The participants in the 2017 study were all self-reported aphantasiacs; they were seemingly unable to conjure up mental images. The study found that people with aphantasia, unlike people in the general population, were barely influenced by the priming task prior to the binocular display. These results provide objective evidence that aphantasia is a genuine condition in which the mind is seemingly unable to conjure up mental images.

13
THE BLAME GAME

Research Areas:

MORALITY   PERCEPTION

 **The experiment**

Together, you should read the paragraph below, then answer the questions that follow.

> Kenny and Dennis are two men who work as cooks in
> a restaurant. When Kenny was in college, he started
> a charity organization that raised money for under-
> privileged kids. While Dennis was in college, he was
> hit and injured by a drunk driver while riding his bike,
> but he has long since recovered. Last week, a woman
> who was severely allergic to almonds ordered an
> almond-free salad. The server placed an allergy alert
> on the order, so the cooks would know that it needed

to be specially prepared. Both Kenny and Dennis should have noticed the allergy alert on the order, but they negligently allowed the salad to be prepared with almonds, and the woman experienced a reaction that required an immediate trip to the ER. The woman told the restaurant's owner that she will sue the restaurant unless the worker responsible is fired.

1. If you had to choose one of the men, Kenny or Dennis, which one should be held more responsible for causing the woman's allergic reaction?
2. If you were the owner and had to choose one of the men, Kenny or Dennis, to fire, whom would it be?

The hypothesis

You and your spouse will assign more blame to Kenny, the man who started the charity when he was in college.

The research

Participants in a 2011 study were presented with a similar scenario about an incident of negligence in a restaurant, but the descriptions of the two cooks varied. Sometimes one of the cooks was portrayed as a hero (such as having founded a children's charity), sometimes as a victim (such as having been hit by a drunk driver), and sometimes as a neutral character (such as having worked in a hardware store). The participants were then asked which of the two cooks bore more responsibility for causing the allergic reaction, and which should be punished with dismissal.

The study's authors found that when one of the cooks was portrayed as a victim, he was assigned less blame than either a hero or a neutral character. And when one of the cooks was portrayed as a hero, he was assigned more blame than either a victim or a neutral character. The researchers think heroes are assigned more blame than a neutral character, and victims are assigned less blame than a neutral character, because we tend to assign blame based on two factors: agency, which they describe as a capacity to make willful choices, and experience, described as a capacity to feel emotions. The more we are perceived to have agency, the more likely we are to be found blameworthy. Experience, on the other hand, appears to be inversely related to blame.

If that's true, then it's consistent with the results of this experiment. Typically, when a person is described as a hero, their agency is emphasized; they made a conscious choice to do something admirable. On the other hand, when a person is described as a victim, their agency is downplayed (because they did not choose to be a victim), while their experience is emphasized.

(!) The takeaway

If you're in hot water with your spouse, or with anyone else for that matter, you may feel as if emphasizing your admirable qualities and your past good deeds might help get you out of it. But the results of this research suggest that this strategy is more likely to land you on the sofa for a few nights. And while people characterized as victims got off easy in this highly constrained experiment, that doesn't mean that claiming victimhood as a defense is going to work for you, particularly not when your spouse knows you well enough to judge the flimsiness of your excuse. Remember, you're in this marriage for the long haul, and the best way to ensure lasting happiness is to skip the excuses and fess up when you mess up.

14
TRIP THE SCRIPT

Research Areas:
COGNITION   EMOTIONS   MEMORY

 The experiment

Flip a coin to determine which spouse will be in the "Awe-Inspiring" condition and which spouse will be in the "Dull" condition. Each of you should separately spend five to ten minutes viewing online content (such as images or videos) that fit your assigned condition. For instance, the person in the "Awe-Inspiring" condition might browse through images of outer space that reveal the vastness of the cosmos, while the person in the "Dull" condition might watch a video about how to re-grout bathroom tiles.

After you have viewed the content that befits your condition, you should each read the following story:

Mike felt nervous during the drive into the city. He and Deanna had reserved a table at Ristorante Divino to celebrate their first month of marriage— what Deanna called their "month-iversary"—and he hoped the romantic atmosphere and the time together as a couple might help her unwind and forget about their current living arrangements.

Six weeks before their wedding, they had been days away from closing on a house when the deal fell through. Hunting for a house while juggling last-minute wedding preparations made for a stressful lead-up to their vows, and although their honeymoon provided a welcome respite, it was short-lived. After they arrived home, they moved in with Deanna's parents. They were grateful for the hospitality, but they felt awkward living under her parents' roof and were anxious to have a home to call their own.

Two days ago, they'd put in an offer for a house in an up-and-coming neighborhood not far from their jobs, but since then, they'd heard nothing back from their real estate agent, Karen, a friend of

Deanna's mother. Mike could tell that Deanna was worried the offer would be rejected.

When they arrived at the restaurant, a valet opened the door for Deanna and assisted her out of the car, then walked around to the driver's side, where Mike handed him the keys and the valet handed him a claim ticket.

Inside the restaurant, they approached the front desk. A short man with a bushy mustache stood behind it, idly arranging a stack of folded napkins. Mike gave the man their name, and he found it on a reservations list and ushered them into the dining area. Swiftly, he led them to a square table for two in a quiet corner of the restaurant.

After sitting down, Deanna reached into her purse, dug around for her cell phone, then placed it on the table. To Mike, it was an unwelcome intruder. He had a feeling that if the phone remained on the table, he would be competing with it for Deanna's attention for most of the meal.

"Tell you what," he said, taking her hand. "Let's make this a phone-free dinner. I know you're anxious to hear about the house, but I think we could both use this time to forget about everything else and concentrate on us."

She gazed at him and realized he was right. She needed this time with Mike, and she knew the phone would only be a distraction.

She summoned the willpower to pick up the phone and toss it back into her purse.

As they looked over the menu, a man dressed all in black introduced himself as their waiter and filled their glasses with water from a large carafe.

Mike, hoping to lift Deanna's mood, ordered a celebratory bottle of wine. The waiter also took their dinner orders. Mike ordered salmon. Deanna ordered a salad.

The waiter put on a pained expression. "Only a salad?"

Deanna laughed. "I need to save room for dessert. It's a special occasion."

The waiter winked and said, "I approve!"

He shuffled off to the kitchen to put in their order.

As she looked around the restaurant, Deanna noticed a painting hanging on the wall whose style was unmistakably that of Leonid Afremov. With thick, bright strokes of oil paint, it depicted a couple holding an umbrella as they strolled through a park on a rainy evening. Deanna's father had bought a similar Afremov painting for her mother on her birthday two years ago, and it had been displayed above the mantel in their living room ever since.

Deanna loved Afremov's style and considered the painting one of the most beautiful things in her parents' house, but seeing the Afremov in the restaurant reminded her that after their romantic dinner, they would be returning back to a guest room in her parents' house, not to a house of their own. She sighed.

When their meals arrived, the couple's conversation began to pick up. They talked about their wedding, their honeymoon, their jobs, their hopes for the future—

A muffled ringing sound emanated from Deanna's purse.

She looked at Mike with wide eyes. He knew how eager she was to hear news about the house. But she knew how important it was to him to wait until the meal was over. She resisted the urge to answer the phone. The ringing continued, then stopped. The call had gone to voicemail.

As he was finishing his salmon, Mike accidentally dropped his fork, and as it fell, it splashed a few drops of oil onto his shirt. He quickly got up, found the men's restroom, and wiped off his shirt.

When he returned, Deanna had a guilty look on her face.

"I know you wanted to have a phone-free dinner," she said, embarrassed. "But I caved."

"Well, what's the news?" he asked.

She shook her head. "It was just a call from my parents."

"Anything important?"

"I didn't check the message," she said. "It can wait."

Their waiter stopped by with more water and a dessert menu.

The chocolate torte and tiramisu both looked tasty, but since this was their "month-iversary" dinner, they agreed to split a lemon cake that reminded them of their wedding cake.

After dessert and while waiting for the check, Mike encouraged Deanna to check the message from her parents, just in case it was important.

Deanna listened to the voicemail, and her mouth fell open.

"We got it!" she said.

"The house?" Mike asked.

"Yes! Karen, the Realtor, left a message on my parents' home phone, thinking that we were there. And get this—they didn't even counter. They agreed to the price we offered!"

"That's incredible," Mike said. "Makes me want to go out to a fancy Italian restaurant and eat cake to celebrate."

Deanna smiled and clutched Mike's hands.

After paying, they walked toward the front door, arm in arm, and the same short man who had greeted them when they arrived asked them if they had used the valet service. Mike produced his valet claim slip. The man picked up the handset of a black telephone and asked the valet to bring the car around.

"First time here?" he asked as Mike and Deanna waited for their car.

"Yes," Deanna said. "The food was wonderful."

"Delighted to hear that," the man said. "Was this a special occasion for you? A birthday?"

"Our month-iversary," Deanna said.

The little man looked at her blankly.

"One month since our wedding day," Mike clarified.

The man smiled a broad smile. "May it be the first of many 'month-iversaries,'" he said. "And may you come back here to celebrate every one."

Now that you've read the story together, it's time to answer some questions about what happened. But to make the task a little more challenging, take about ten minutes to distract yourselves: play a board game, make out, or balance your checkbooks. Once you've been sufficiently distracted, come back and answer these "true or false" questions about the story:

Mike was the driver and Deanna the passenger during the ride to the restaurant. (T/F)

The parking valet had a bushy mustache. (T/F)

The couple sat at a candlelit table with a white table-
cloth. (T/F)

In the painting that Deanna recognized, a woman
holding an umbrella was strolling through the park.
(T/F)

Deanna's father gave a painting by Leonid Afremov to
his wife as a gift. (T/F)

Mike and Deanna both ordered fish as their entrées.
(T/F)

The couple's real estate agent was a friend of
Deanna's mother. (T/F)

Mike visited the men's restroom to clean a spill off his
tie. (T/F)

After dinner, a waitress stopped by with a dessert
menu. (T/F)

The man at the front desk directed the valet to retrieve
the couple's car. (T/F)

Now, turn to page 244 to check your answers.

The hypothesis

The spouse who was in the "Awe-Inspiring" condition will answer more of the true/false questions correctly than the spouse who was in the "Dull" condition.

The research

Awe is a "direct and initial feeling when faced with something incomprehensible or sublime," according to a 2015 study of how astronauts experience awe and wonder during space missions. We tend to feel awe when we suddenly become aware of how small or insignificant we are compared with something or someone else. We might feel awed as we gaze upon something majestic, like a mountain or an ocean, or consider things that are eternal, boundless, perfect, or transcendent: God, the universe, the golden ratio, or Katie Couric. But aside from keeping us humble, does awe affect us in other, more unexpected ways?

The authors of a 2017 study showed some participants awe-inspiring footage of space, while others watched a dull tutorial on how to build a cinder-block wall. They then listened to a five-minute story about a couple going out to dinner. After completing an unrelated distractor task, they were quizzed about the story. Some of the questions had to do with details that were script-typical, meaning they were consistent with typical things that happen during a restaurant experience. Other questions had to do with details that were script-independent, or not directly relevant to a "dining out" script.

The researchers found that the participants who'd watched the awe-inspiring footage did a better job than participants in the dull-footage condition at identifying script-typical details that were false, and script-independent details that were true. (Women, it should be mentioned, did better than men across conditions.)

Why might awe have this effect on memory? The researchers suggest that in a state of awe, our minds open a bit wider than normal, and as a result, we rely less on our usual expectations. Or, to put it another way: when we're in the presence of something magical, we realize that the regular rules might not apply, so we abandon our scripts and pay attention to what things actually are, rather than what we expect them to be.

(!) The takeaway

As an emotion, awe is pretty unique. One of its main effects is to make us strongly aware of our smallness and insignificance, which would ordinarily make it seem like a bedfellow of negative emotions like humiliation. Yet we tend to instead perceive awe as a positive emotion, one that we actively seek out. And this research indicates that beyond being a pleasurable emotion, awe also helps us better see things as they really are. So look for ways that you and your partner can experience awe in your travels, in your day-to-day life, and in your relationship. Seek out nature's wonders, profound artistic works, and once-in-a-lifetime experiences. But also try to cultivate a sense of awe about everyday life. With the right mindset, you can marvel at the mere fact that you're you, or that you and your spouse happened to find each other, or that atoms that make up a dull cinder-block wall might have emanated from some unfathomably far-off star in the galaxy billions of years ago.

15
ON A POSITIVE NOTE

Research Areas:

RELATIONSHIP   SOCIAL
QUALITY   PSYCHOLOGY

🧪 The experiment

Cut a standard letter-sized sheet of paper (8.5 by 11 inches) into four equal-sized strips, so that each strip is 11 inches long. Use a ruler to draw a straight, 10-inch line on each of the strips. Draw small hatches at the bottom, middle, and top of the line, and write labels "B" and "T" at the bottom and top, respectively.

Flip a coin to decide which of you will be the Interviewer and which of you will be the Storyteller. Storyteller, think of three events that made you happiest over the past two years, such as a honeymoon, a great concert, a religious conversion, or a recovery from an illness. Rank those three events in terms of how happy each made you. Then, for the second- and third-ranked events, select a strip and label it on the back

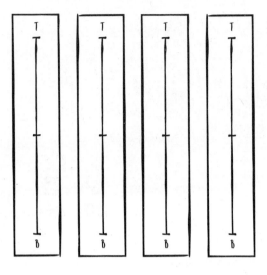

with the item name, along with the word "BEFORE." For your second-ranked event, make a mark on the line to rate how happy it made you, using a scale where the bottom hatch mark represents "pretty good," the middle hatch mark represents "great," and the top hatch mark represents "the best thing that ever happened to me." Set that strip aside so that you can't see the rating you gave it, and then, on the strip associated with the third-ranked event, rate how happy it made you using the same scale.

Flip a coin again to determine which of the two rated events is going to be the Focus Event. You are going to spend about five minutes telling your spouse, the Interviewer, the details of this event: how and when it started, some of the things about the event that made you the happiest, and its lasting impact.

Before you begin recounting the event, the Interviewer should turn to page 244 for special instructions.

Storyteller, once you're finished recounting the Focus Event, it's time to use the remaining strips of paper to re-rate your second- and third-ranked events. For both events, select a strip and label it on the back with the item name, along with the word "AFTER." Then, without comparing any of the strips, re-rate how happy each event made you, according to the same scale you used before.

Finally, line up the four strips of paper, get out your ruler, and measure each rating.

🄿 The hypothesis

The difference between your two ratings of the Focus Event (before and after talking to your spouse about it) will be greater than the difference between your two ratings of the other event.

🔬 The research

It's natural for us to want to share good news and positive events with other people. Researchers in a 2010 study wanted to test whether the process of sharing those events increases the perceived value of the events. They conducted an experiment in which participants selected significant events that had happened in the previous two years. They rated each of the events both before and after recounting one of the events to the Interviewer, who had been instructed to provide positive, enthusiastic feedback.

The study found that receiving active, constructive feedback while sharing a positive event increased the participants' rating of the event, compared with the positive event they did not share. This effect was not seen in control conditions, such as writing privately about the event, and it was also not seen when the verbal and nonverbal feedback was passive and aloof. In subsequent experiments, the study's authors also found that when a participant shared a positive event with someone who responded with positive, enthusiastic support, it led the participant to like and trust the other person more.

(!) The takeaway

Your spouse is probably the first person you want to share good news with. The results of this study show that how your spouse responds to that good news can affect not only your perception of its value, but also the intimacy of your relationship. With that in mind, when either of you shares good news with the other, give your spouse your full attention, demonstrate active listening skills, and let them know how genuinely happy you are for them. Not only will it enhance their own perception of the event, but it will also likely enhance their perception of you.

WHY NOTCHES?

In this experiment, you rated your feelings about the happy events you recalled by drawing a mark on a line that represented a scale. But why were you instructed to draw your rating, rather than just write down a number from 1 to 10, as you did in many of the other experiments in this book? The researchers who designed the experiment wanted to make sure that the second time the participants rated the experiences, they weren't just recalling their original ratings, which would have been easy to do if they had been asked to give numeric ratings. Asking the participants to draw a mark on a physical line helped ensure that each time they rated the events, they could do so on a continuum (rather than on an integer scale), and in such a way that the memory of a previous rating would be less likely to influence their current rating.

PART 3

TRY A CHALLENGE

16
A BENEVOLENT NUDGE

Research Areas: BEHAVIOR MORALITY

The experiment

Flip a coin to decide which spouse will complete a geography challenge and which will complete a religion challenge. The spouse in the geography condition should attempt to write down the names of the ten U.S. cities with the highest population. The other spouse should attempt to write down as many of the Ten Commandments as they can recall.

Next, each of you should rate, on a scale from 1 to 10, the degree to which you consider the following labels to be central to your identity:

A. a successful person ____
B. a hardworking person ____

C. a generous person _____

D. an independent person _____

E. a compassionate person _____

Finally, both spouses should consider the following scenario:

You are the marketing manager of a cereal company that awards year-end bonuses based on profit targets. You are considering a proposal to donate 25 cents to a children's cancer charity for each product purchased. You've determined that if you implement this proposal, you will be less likely to hit the profit target required to receive a bonus. How likely, on a scale from 1 to 10, are you to implement the proposal?

🔮 The hypothesis

The spouse who had to list the Ten Commandments is more likely to implement the proposal to donate to the children's cancer charity. This is most likely to hold true if the spouse did not give high ratings for labels B, C, and E.

⚗️ The experiment

It's long been known that our propensity for making moral choices depends, in part, on the situation. You might, for instance, feel more inclined to act in a virtuous way if you are aware that someone you wish to impress is observing you. But there is another factor that appears to influence moral behavior, and rather than vacillating with the situation, it's more or less a stable characteristic: our moral identity. If a person considers their moral identity to be central to their sense of self, they are likely to behave in ways that are consistent with that self-image. If a person instead considers other facets of their identity to be more fundamental to their sense of self, their behaviors are less likely to be influenced by their moral identity.

Researchers in a 2009 study were curious about the interplay between situational factors and moral identity. They devised an experiment in which a control group of subjects were asked about geography, while those in the experiment group were given a "moral priming" task (recalling and reviewing the Ten Commandments).

Then the subjects were given a list of attributes and asked to identify which ones were most central to their identity.

Finally, they were presented with a scenario similar to the children's cancer charity scenario you and your partner considered, and they were asked how likely they would be to implement the proposal and potentially sacrifice a year-end bonus.

The study's results showed that when a situational factor, such as the "moral priming" task, activated a person's sense of moral identity, they were more likely to engage in benevolent behavior, such as being willing to put personal gain aside to help a worthy cause.

But the degree to which the moral priming task influenced people's behavior was not uniform. It had a stronger effect on people who had a relatively weak sense of moral identity and a lesser effect on people who had a relatively high sense of moral identity. Why would that be? The study's authors suggest that when our moral identity is not central to our sense of self, situational factors, such as the moral priming task, have more power to activate that identity, to make it more accessible to our present self-concept, and to nudge that identity closer to the front of our minds. But when our moral identity is already central to our sense of self, situational factors have less influence, because that identity is already activated and highly accessible to our present self-concept.

(!) The takeaway

There will assuredly be times in your marriage when you will need to engage in self-sacrificing behavior. You may need to pass up on personal gain or pleasure for the benefit of your spouse, or other members of your family, or for some greater societal good. And when your moral identity is either at the center of your overall identity, or it's pushed toward the center by situational factors, you become more likely to engage in that benevolent, pro-social behavior.

The experiment you just completed used a rather subtle, indirect method of activating that moral identity, but you and your spouse need not be that subtle in your own efforts. You can directly remind yourself that you are a person who considers exhibiting moral qualities as important and that you hold yourself to high moral standards.

One other point to take away is that just as positive situational factors can influence those who have a relatively weak sense of moral identity, so too can negative situational factors influence those who have a relatively high sense of moral identity. They can lead us to make immoral or self-serving choices, and they can also weaken that enduring sense of identity. So don't assume that just because you have a relatively strong sense of moral identity, you are immune to temptation or change. Maintaining your moral identity as a central part of who you are isn't automatic; it requires continued effort.

17

MENTAL PICTURES

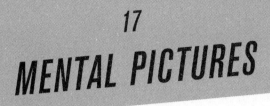

<table>
<tr><td>Research Areas:</td><td></td></tr>
</table>

Research Areas: 🌐 👁
LANGUAGE   PERCEPTION

 ## The experiment

You'll need a stopwatch for this project. Flip a coin to decide who will be the Timekeeper. Now, Timekeeper, read the following eight sentences to your spouse:

> I put the pencil in the cup.
>
> The eagle sat in its nest.
>
> The baby sat in its high chair.
>
> The book stood in the bookcase.
>
> A mannequin stood in a store window.
>
> Put the toothpaste onto the toothbrush.
>
> The egg was inside the carton.
>
> The flowers were displayed in a vase.

Next, the Timekeeper should show, one by one, each of the pictures on page 245, and prompt your spouse to state whether the object shown in the picture was mentioned in any of the sentences. For each picture, start the stopwatch the instant you reveal the image and end it when your spouse gives a response.

The hypothesis

Of the six pictures, only four depict objects that were mentioned in the sentences. They are the pictures of the pencil, the eagle, the egg, and the book. Your partner will respond faster for the pictures of the pencil and the egg than for the pictures of the eagle and the book.

The research

How do we mentally represent the concepts that are expressed through language? Consider these two sentences: *The egg was in the carton* and *The egg was in the frying pan*. Some language comprehension researchers might say that our mental representation of "the egg" is essentially the same in both cases. But a 2001 study found that our mental representations of the same object might vary based on the context.

Participants were given sentences in which a horizontal

or vertical orientation of an object was implied. For instance, *I put the pencil in the cup* implies that the pencil is vertically oriented, but *I put the pencil on the table* implies that the pencil is horizontally oriented. The participants were later shown pictures of objects that either matched or did not match the implied orientation, and the subjects were able to more quickly identify which objects had been mentioned in the sentences when the orientation of the pictures was the same as the implied orientation in the sentences.

A 2002 follow-up study examined whether not just the orientation of an object but also its general shape might be encoded in our mental representations. An eagle sitting in its nest, for instance, has a different shape than an eagle soaring in the sky. The results showed that response times were again quicker when the shape of the object depicted in the images matched the shape of the object implied by the sentences.

And a 2009 study confirmed that these findings hold true even when the images aren't shown directly after each sentence, but are instead shown after all the sentences have been read, as they were in the adapted experiment you and your spouse just performed.

The results give weight to the idea that our mental

representations of objects and concepts are dynamic and contextualized, rather than merely an assembly of static mental images.

(!) The takeaway

It's bad enough that communication problems can occur because of linguistic quirks like homophones and ambiguous pronouns. For instance, if your partner is waiting for you to exit the bathroom and knocks on the door, shouting "Coming, honey" might sound a lot like "Come in, honey"—but the meaning is very different. Or if you say to your spouse, "When I dropped the hammer on my finger, it broke!" you might get driven to the hardware store instead of the hospital.

The results of this research show that in addition to those cases, how you mentally represent concepts—even if you and your spouse are on the same page about what those concepts are—can also lead to misunderstandings. For example, imagine you're on a hike and your spouse, a few yards ahead, says, "Watch out for those branches." You might instinctively look up, hoping to avoid bumping into low-hanging tree branches above, but instead, you might end up tripping over a jumble of fallen branches on the ground below. The best way to survive these perceptual mix-ups is to employ a two-pronged approach: a high level of communication with your spouse to reduce the likelihood of confusion and a willingness to let occasional misunderstandings slide.

18
MISS QUOTA

 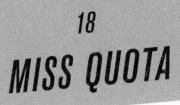
The experiment

Flip a coin to decide who will be Contestant A and who will be Contestant B in a jumbled-letters game. Contestant A, read the instructions on page 246. Contestant B, read the instructions on page 254.

After you have each read your respective instructions, set five minutes on a timer and begin the game, using the five sets of jumbled letters below:

CISNCONINYSTE   USIURTRAETRNFC

EMOLMYUNNTAL   LWAMCNEOKEDETNG

CLOGAISTRNOMA

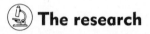 The hypothesis

Contestant B is more likely than Contestant A to have fudged their score.

The research

In a 2010 study, researchers investigated how people misrepresent their performance under various compensation systems. Participants were given an opportunity to earn money in a jumbled-letter task similar to the one you completed. Some of the participants were told they'd earn a certain amount of money for every dictionary word they identified, while others were told they would only earn a payout if they reached a certain performance target.

The study found that the participants in the target-based group were significantly more likely to misrepresent the number of words they had identified. In fact, the average number of overclaimed words by those in the target-based group was more than two and a half times the average number of overclaimed words by those who earned points for every word. The researchers note, however, that one of the biggest cheaters in the study was a member of the per-word group. So even though the target-based compensation system seems to tempt more people to cheat than the other systems studied, brazen cheating can occur in any setting.

(!) The takeaway

There will likely be times during your marriage when you feel tempted to fudge the truth. On the more innocuous side, it might be "Your lasagna is way better than my mother's," or "I have no preference where in the room that sofa goes." But lying about something serious to your spouse, such as reconnecting with an old flame or financial debt that's spun out of control, can threaten your marriage. One way to keep yourself honest is to remember that in many cases, your word isn't the only record of the truth, and if your spouse stumbles onto evidence, such as a receipt or a letter, that contradicts your account, you will have some explaining to do. Also, remember that small lies often beget bigger lies, so unless you want your relationship to crumble down, keep everything on the up-and-up.

CHUGGING CHALLENGE

🧪 The experiment

For this project, you'll need to agree on a small reward and a larger reward, such as a scoop of ice cream on your next outing together for the small reward and a giant sundae with multiple toppings for the larger reward. You'll also need to gather two large containers, one for each of you, and fill each container with three pints (1.4 liters) of water. Finally, you'll need a stopwatch or timer.

Flip a coin to decide which of you will be Chugger A and which of you will be Chugger B. You will each be given the opportunity to

win a reward by drinking all the water in your container within two minutes.

Chugger A should read the additional instructions on page 246, and Chugger B should read the additional instructions on page 254. Once you've both finished reading, set the timer and try to complete the challenge!

The hypothesis

Chugger B is more likely than Chugger A to complete the challenge.

The research

Does uncertainty about the value of a reward increase or decrease motivation? That was the question explored in a series of experiments conducted as part of a 2014 study.

In one of those experiments, participants performed the same challenge you just performed, drinking three pints of water within two minutes. One group of participants was told that they would receive $2 for completing the challenge, while another group was told that they would earn either $1 or $2, determined by a coin flip, for completing it.

Among the participants who knew they would receive $2, only 43 percent completed the challenge. But among those who had an equal chance of receiving either $1 or $2, 70 percent completed the challenge! In follow-up experiments, the researchers found that uncertainty motivated people more than certainty, even when the probability of receiving the larger reward was made significantly lower than 50 percent.

The researchers note that these results appear to contradict previous research, which demonstrated that an uncertain outcome is typically considered a negative factor in decision-making. That makes sense, because who among us, when offered the choice between either a certain $100 reward or a reward where $50 and $100 are equally likely, would opt for the latter? The researchers explain this discrepancy by pointing out that uncertainty might be a negative factor when the focus is on the rewards themselves, but it appears to be a positive, motivating factor when the focus is on the process of obtaining a reward, as with the chugging challenge.

ⓘ The takeaway

We all get a certain thrill out of uncertainty, particularly when the thing we are uncertain about is something positive, like a prize. Not knowing for certain what reward we might receive inspires excitement and increases our level of effort in trying to earn the reward. No wonder prize wheels are so popular! You might want to factor this in when you decide whether to introduce a sense of uncertainty as you plan your next night out with your spouse, or as you come up with a reward for some personal achievement, such as hitting an exercise goal. It might seem like a sure-thing sundae is the best motivator, but the thrill of the unknown might, in fact, give you all the motivation you need.

MAYBE IT'S LOVE

Uncertainty appears to affect not only motivation but also preferences. For instance, in a 2011 study, female college students were shown pictures of four male college students who had purportedly viewed their Facebook profile and indicated their level of interest in the women. As you might expect, the women were more likely to be interested in the men who appeared more interested in them. But when the women were shown a profile of a man who was said to have either rated her very highly, or given her an average rating, the women's level of interest spiked even higher than in the case where they knew for certain that the man had expressed a high level of interest!

20
DISTORTED TRUTHS

Research Areas: COGNITION LANGUAGE

The experiment

You and your spouse will each be given five trivia questions. Be prepared to write down your answers to the questions in the spaces provided, or on separate slips of paper. You may or may not encounter questions that are ill-formed and can't be answered if taken literally. Please write "Can't say" for these questions. If you don't know the answer, write "Don't know." Answer the questions as quickly and accurately as you can; it shouldn't take you more than one minute to answer all five questions.

Flip a coin to decide who will answer the first round of questions. That spouse should turn to page 247 and begin. Once that person has finished, the other partner should turn to page 255 and begin.

❓ The hypothesis

The spouse who completed the first round of questions, which were presented in a hard-to-read font, is more likely to have answered "Can't say" for the first, third, and fourth questions than the spouse who completed the second round of questions, which were presented in an easy-to-read font.

🔬 The research

Researchers have been studying what's known as the Moses Illusion since it was first introduced in a 1981 study that examined how we extract meaning from individual words. In that study, the authors found that when people were asked, "How many of each animal did Moses take on the ark?" most people responded, "Two," even though they were aware that it was Noah, and not Moses, who was the central character in the biblical story of the ark. The effect persisted even when subjects were informed ahead of time that the question might be ill-formed.

The experiment you and your spouse performed is modeled after a 2008 study in which versions of the Moses Illusion were presented to two groups of participants. One group read the questions in an easy-to-read font, and the other read them in a difficult-to-read font. The study found that those in the difficult-font group were more likely to identify the ill-formed questions. The study's authors believe that when it is easy to process a sentence, we are more likely to treat an aberrant word (such as "Moses") as if it were the appropriate word (such as "Noah"), because easily processed sentences are more likely to seem familiar and less likely to be scrutinized, so people tend to respond with the first answer that comes to mind. In contrast, hard-to-process material engages more of our mental resources and reduces our confidence, which might lead us to second-guess the answer that springs to mind.

(!) The takeaway

It may seem counterintuitive, but the results of this research suggest that at least in certain cases, it's easier to hide an aberrant word in plain sight than by obscuring the message using a difficult-to-process presentation format. Or, to put it more broadly, the less engaged our brain needs to be to understand the message, the more likely we are to fail to notice inconsistencies or distortions. Multitasking is often the culprit here. Think about the times when your spouse has misunderstood something you said or wrote because they were simultaneously watching a TV show or browsing a website. In times when it's really important that your spouse understands precisely what you're saying, you might apply this principle by, for instance, speaking in a slower-than-normal voice during verbal communication, or by boldfacing or underlining important written words that might otherwise be mentally skipped over.

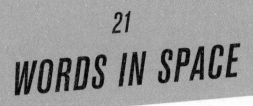

21

WORDS IN SPACE

> **Research Areas:** COGNITION   MEMORY

🧪 The experiment

Flip a coin to determine who will be the Instructor and who will be the Memorizer. Only the Instructor should read on.

You are going to help the Memorizer commit to memory the following list of ten words in the order in which they appear:

DOG   ORANGE   MUG   SOFA   PENCIL

HOUSE   VAN   MIRROR   NAIL   COIN

You can help the Memorizer with this task by repeating the list a few times, then reciting the list word by word while they repeat each word back to you. Once you are satisfied that the Memorizer has committed the words to memory and can recite all ten items in the correct order, move on to the next step.

Sit at a table opposite the Memorizer and tell them that you are going to read a few words from the list. If a word is from the first half of the list, they should tap the table with their *left* hand; if it is from the second half of the list, they should tap the table with their *right* hand.

As you read the following words, use a stopwatch to record how long it takes your spouse to tap the table: *house, coin, mug, van, orange*.

Next, tell your spouse that you are going to read the remaining words from the list, but this time, if a word is from the first half of the list, they should tap the table with their *right* hand, and if it's from the second half of the list, they should tap the table with their *left* hand.

Again, as you read the following words, use a stopwatch to record how long it takes your spouse to tap the table: *pencil, dog, sofa, nail, mirror*.

⊕ The hypothesis

For each set of test words, your spouse will be slower to tap the table if the words are closer to the middle of the list. Additionally, your spouse will have slower response times for the second set of test words than for the first set.

🔬 The research

When people mentally represent sequences that have a particular order, such as numbers, days of the week, or months of a year, those representations tend to be spatial, meaning we envision the sequences flowing in a particular direction, such as from left to right. In a 2010 study, researchers devised a way to determine whether sequences of words that had no innate order associated with them, such as a random list of common nouns, are represented in the same way.

In their experiment, participants memorized a list of words and were then shown the words on a computer screen and had to identify, by pressing a key with either their left or right hand, whether each word was from the first half of the list or the second half. The researchers then examined the participants' reaction times. They found that left-handed responses were faster for words in the first half, but right-handed responses were faster for words in the second half. In fact, the farther the word was from the middle, the more pronounced the effect was. These results, the researchers concluded, are indicative of a spatial mental representation of list items, and not just items that have a learned order to them (such as days of the week), but any ordered sequence.

A similar effect is seen when numbers, rather than words, are used. At least in Western cultures, where the number line is generally represented in a left-to-right fashion, people tend to respond quicker with their left hand when the number is small, but quicker with their right hand when the number is large. Thus, it appears that the left-to-right spatial association holds true not only for the order of unrelated items in a list but also for the magnitude of numbers. A 2014 study explored whether a person's mathematical proficiency might influence this effect. It found that participants with relatively poor mathematical skills exhibited the effect strongly, while people with relatively good mathematical skills exhibited the effect more weakly. The researchers think that people with strong math skills are better able to disregard irrelevant information, such as the magnitude of the numbers.

(I) **The takeaway**

Think about the lists you and your spouse regularly compose: grocery lists, guest lists, playlists, wish lists, and to-do lists. The items in these lists might not have any intrinsic order, but your brain nevertheless treats them as if they fall somewhere on a spatial continuum when you hold them in memory. Why does it do this? Likely as a memory aid, a sort of subconscious mnemonic system that helps you remember the order of your lists. On the one hand, take a moment to marvel at how awesome it is that your brain can do this for you without any conscious effort. On the other hand, unless you've got a photographic memory, you should probably write down that to-do list, just in case.

22

TEMPTING YOUR IMPULSES

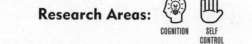

Research Areas: COGNITION SELF CONTROL

The experiment

Flip a coin to decide which of you will be the Prize Purchaser. That person should read on.

You'll need to take a trip to the supermarket to pick up the prizes that will be used as part of this experiment. Select two small slices of chocolate cake, or a similarly decadent dessert, as well as two containers of fruit salad that are similar in price to the cake slices. Once you've purchased the prizes, cover them up on a table so that your spouse is not able to see them. Next, each of you should write down a random seven-digit number on a slip of paper. Exchange your slips of paper and read the following instructions out loud:

Each of you should memorize the number written on the

slip of paper you were given. Your goal is to keep this number in your head while engaging in a two-minute distracting activity, such as listening to music. You will then walk over to the prize table and uncover the prizes, which consist of two food options. Choose which option you would like to receive if you've managed to keep the correct number in memory. Once each of you has made your prize selection, announce the number you've memorized, and if you were correct, enjoy your prize! (If you weren't correct, enjoy the prize on another day.)

⍰ The hypothesis

The Prize Purchaser is more likely to select the fruit salad, but the other spouse is more likely to select the chocolate cake.

🔬 The research

Chocolate cake might be delicious, but it's not so good for your waistline, or your health in general. In contrast, fruit salad might be a healthier treat, but it's hardly considered decadent.

Researchers in a 2002 study understood that when we act on our more basic impulses, we're more likely to go for the cake, but when we use our higher-level faculties and consider the healthfulness of the options, we're more likely to select the fruit. They devised an experiment to see what factors might influence us to lean one way or the other. They divided participants into several groups, who had to maintain a seven-digit number in memory while doing a distracting task. Some of the participants were able to see and deliberate about the snacks during those two minutes, while others didn't get to see the snacks until they approached the prize table.

The researchers found that when participants had less time to deliberate about their decision, about 50 percent chose the chocolate cake as their prize. Participants who had sufficient time to deliberate, however, chose the chocolate cake only about 37 percent of the time. Interestingly, when participants had to memorize a two-digit number instead of a seven-digit number, and so were operating under lower cognitive load, the percentages flip-flopped. Those with less time to deliberate chose the cake 30 percent of the time, versus 56 percent of the time when the prizes were in full view during the distraction task.

The results of this study suggest that when we have only a short time to make a decision, anything that increases our cognitive load makes us more susceptible to acting on our impulses, but if we have a long time to make a decision, things that decrease our cognitive load will also lead us to make decisions that appeal to our baser appetites.

(!) The takeaway

Decisions about purchases occur frequently within a marriage, and when spouses disagree about those decisions, it can cause strain in their relationships, not to mention pain in their wallets. To protect both your financial and relationship health, it's important for both spouses to be mindful about marketing techniques that are designed to separate you from your money. For instance, stores might blast distracting music or use flashy displays in an effort to increase your cognitive load and decrease your resistance to an impulse purchase. On the other hand, if you have a long time to decide on a purchase (such as a vacation package), promotions that encourage low cognitive load (such as sitting through a boring marketing presentation before choosing from among several available options) might entice you or your spouse to make a more impulsive buy. The best way for you to guard against this kind of marketing manipulation is to be aware of it—and to remind your partner to be aware of it as well.

23

KARAOKE CHALLENGE

Research Areas: CONSTRUAL   EMOTIONS

🧪 The experiment

It's your lucky day! Not only is this project a science experiment, but it's also a great date night idea! You'll need to search your local event listings for a karaoke night at a local restaurant or bar and commit yourselves to performing at least one song each. Bring this book along with you, and while you're waiting for your turn at the microphone, flip a coin to decide who will be Singer A and who will be Singer B. Singer A should read the instructions on page 247. Singer B should read the instructions on page 255. Now, sing your hearts out!

After each of you has had an opportunity to perform a song, answer the following questions on a scale from 1 (very low) to 10 (very high):

What was your level of anxiety while performing? ____

What was your level of excitement while performing?

____

How confident did you feel while performing? ____

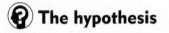

The hypothesis

Singer A, who read instructions that reframed anxiety as a performance-boosting response to stress, is likely to report having been more excited and more confident than Singer B. And if you and your spouse's singing abilities are similar, Singer A is likely to have earned a little bit more applause.

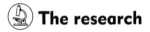

The research

In ordinary speech, the term "arousal" often refers to sexual arousal, but in psychology, it is used more broadly to refer to the various ways in which the body becomes more physically and mentally alert and ready to respond. Anxiety before and during a stressful event, such as performing a song in public, is a type of arousal that can rise well above mere alertness and send our minds and our bodies into a frightened or panicky state, or otherwise affect our ability to perform a task well. But several recent studies have found that it is possible to mitigate the effects of anxiety using a technique called reappraisal.

In one form of reappraisal, feelings of anxiety are described as performance enhancers rather than performance inhibitors. A 2010 study found that this type of reappraisal led to improved performance versus a control group among college students taking a practice test for graduate school admissions. (It also led to improved performance on the math section of the actual test, which they took within three months of the practice test.)

In another form of the technique, feelings of anxiety, a negative emotion, are reinterpreted as feelings of excitement, a positive emotion. In a 2014 study, participants were asked to perform a karaoke song while an experimenter evaluated their singing performance. Participants who had been encouraged to reframe their anxiety as excitement ended up performing better than those who didn't do any reframing. In fact, reinterpreting anxiety as excitement worked even better than encouraging participants to calm down. The study's author suggests that a reframing strategy works better than a calming strategy because in the reframing strategy, one high-arousal emotion is replaced with another high-arousal emotion, which might "trick" the mind better than trying to replace a high-arousal emotion with a low-arousal state.

⚠ The takeaway

Stressful situations, both inside and outside of your marital relationship, can affect your mind, your body, your performance on the task at hand, your emotional state, and your general sense of well-being. One way of coping with those situations is to fool your mind into thinking that the state of high arousal it's experiencing is a positive thing, rather than a negative thing, and the good news is that it's surprisingly easy to do. Even just telling yourself, "I'm excited!" appears to do the trick. Try it the next time your spouse drags you along to a work function where you have to hobnob with strangers! Another way to practice reappraisal is to take criticism from others and try to construe it as constructive rather than as a threat, such as when your in-laws visit and offer unsolicited housekeeping tips. It may help to not only relieve the pit in your stomach but also increase your performance.

EASIER TO ACCEPT

In the previous project, you explored an emotional-regulation strategy known as reappraisal.

Another way to regulate negative emotions is by using an acceptance strategy, where a person accepts the feelings they are experiencing without trying to control or judge them.

A 2018 study examined the pros and cons of each strategy. Participants were assigned to use one of the two strategies while watching sad film clips. The participants who used reappraisal reported a larger decrease in negative emotions, but the participants who used acceptance rated it an easier strategy to use.

The study's authors suggest that reappraisal may be a good first strategy for tackling strong emotional-regulation issues, while acceptance might be a more suitable maintenance strategy over the longer term.

PART 4

CRUNCH THE NUMBERS

24
THE FAIRER SEX?

Research Areas: ECONOMICS GENDER DIFFERENCES

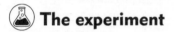 **The experiment**

Each of you will complete the following exercise independently, and then you'll come together to compare your results.

Imagine that you are playing a game to earn money for yourself and a randomly selected attendee of your wedding (or a random Elvis impersonator, if you eloped in Las Vegas).

In the following eight scenarios, you will be given a certain number of tokens, which are each worth a dollar. Your job is to allocate those tokens between yourself and the chosen wedding guest. The guest will have no idea what the scenarios are, what allocations you make, or how much money you earn for yourself.

In some of the scenarios, there will be multipliers assigned to one of the person's tokens, which raise the value of those tokens. For instance, if there is a 2x multiplier on your guest's tokens, then every token your guest receives is doubled in value, meaning it's worth two dollars instead of one dollar. Similarly, if there is a 3x multiplier, then every token your guest receives is tripled in value, meaning it's worth three dollars instead of one dollar.

Here's an example: You're asked to divide ten tokens between yourself and your wedding guest, and there is a 2x multiplier on the tokens your guest receives. You decide to keep five tokens for yourself and give five tokens to the guest. Your five tokens would be worth five dollars, and because of the 2x multiplier on your guest's tokens, their five tokens would be worth ten dollars.

Read through each of these eight scenarios and determine how you will divide the tokens between you and your guest:

1. Divide forty tokens, with a 3x multiplier on the tokens you give to your guest.

2. Divide sixty tokens, with a 2x multiplier on the tokens you give to your guest.

3. Divide seventy-five tokens, with a 2x multiplier on the tokens you give to your guest.

4. Divide sixty tokens, with no multiplier on any of the tokens.

5. Divide a hundred tokens, with no multiplier on any of the tokens.

6. Divide sixty tokens, with a 2x multiplier on the tokens you keep for yourself.

7. Divide seventy-five tokens, with a 2x multiplier on the tokens you keep for yourself.

8. Divide forty tokens, with a 3x multiplier on the tokens you keep for yourself.

Now that you've allocated the tokens, add up the total value of the winnings you've earned for yourself and the total value of the winnings you've earned for your guest.

❓ The hypothesis

If you are like most people, you will probably have kept most of the tokens for yourself, but your sense of generosity and altruism probably led you to give your wedding guest a portion of the tokens in at least some cases. You and your spouse probably ended up with similar total values for the winnings that you allocated to your respective guests. And each of you was probably more generous in the first few scenarios than in the last few. But when you examine some of the individual scenarios, gender differences may become apparent. Men are likely to have been more generous than women in the first few scenarios. Women are likely to have been more generous than men in the last few scenarios.

(🔬) The research

Male and female participants in a 2001 study were asked to perform an allocation task similar to the one described earlier. The results showed that when the scenario was more favorable to oneself (as when the tokens retained had a multiplier applied), men were less generous than women, but when the scenario was more favorable to the recipient (as when tokens given to the recipient had a multiplier applied), men were more generous than women.

This suggests that when it comes to allocating resources, men, on average, might be more sensitive to maximizing total value, whereas women, on average, might be more sensitive to equality. You might call the men's approach a "best bang for your buck" strategy, because it leads them to try to get the highest payout possible, even if it results in a significant difference between what each person receives. And you might call the women's approach a "spread the wealth" strategy, because it leads them to distribute the resources more evenly, even if that means a smaller total payout. For the most part, though, these strategies were blended in with a broader strategy, practiced by both men and women, of retaining most of the tokens for oneself, but exhibiting at least some altruism toward the other person.

The study also uncovered some interesting strategies among subgroups. Men were more likely to be perfectly selfish, keeping all the tokens for themselves in all scenarios. Men were also more likely to use an extreme version of the "best bang for your buck" strategy that maximized the total reward, regardless of who received it, which meant they kept all of the tokens when they had the multiplier and gave away all of the tokens when the recipient had the multiplier.

Behavior consistent with these results can be seen in real-world scenarios. For instance, according to a 2003 study, single men appear to be more sensitive than single women to what might be called subsidized altruism, as is the case with tax deductions for charitable giving. The tax deduction helps stretch the value of each donated dollar in the same way that a multiplier in the experiment helps stretch the value of a token. As a person's tax rate goes up, the value of the deduction also goes up, making charitable giving all the more attractive if you follow a "best bang for your buck" strategy. And indeed, in line with the findings from the token-allocation experiment, the single men in the 2003 study were influenced more by tax incentives for charitable donations than the single women were.

(!) The takeaway

If you plan to jointly make decisions about charitable giving, as many couples do, be aware that you may have different attitudes and propensities toward giving, and you may not always see eye to eye. If, as this research suggests, there are gender differences in the ways people approach altruism, then you'll need to find a way to reconcile those differences to make joint decisions.

You should be aware that the same 2003 study that reported gender differences among single men and women also reported that when heterosexual married couples make joint decisions about charitable giving, the "compromise" they arrive upon tends to incorporate about two-thirds of the husband's preferences and only one-third of the wife's. Being the primary breadwinner and having a higher level of education each boost a spouse's bargaining power, but even in cases where the wife is the higher earner, men tend to have more of a say about charitable giving than women do when their husband is the higher earner.

If you aren't comfortable with an imbalance of power, you may need to lay out some ground rules. For instance, you might agree that regardless of who earned the money, it all goes into one pot, and that each of you gets to determine how half of that pot is allocated.

TIPPING TENDENCIES

In the preceding project, the results suggested that while men seem to be more sensitive to price, women tend to be more sensitive to equality. In 1999, three Cornell researchers examined restaurant tipping behavior and found results consistent with that idea. Although men tended to be better restaurant tippers than women when the bill was relatively small, women tended to be better tippers than men when the bill was relatively large. Or, to put it another way, as the cost of tipping increases, men become less generous, whereas women tend to maintain a more stable tipping percentage regardless of the size of the bill.

25

THE WILL TO WANDER

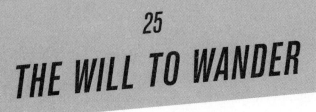

Research Areas:

PERSONALITY   SELF CONTROL

 The experiment

You and your spouse should separately answer the following questions about your personalities. For each question, answer using a scale from 1 (doesn't sound anything like me) to 10 (sounds exactly like me):

A. New ideas or projects sometimes distract me from previous ones. _____

B. Setbacks don't discourage me. I don't give up easily.

_____

C. After an initial burst of enthusiasm in a project, I tend to lose interest. _____

D. I have overcome obstacles to complete an
    important task. _____

E. I often find my thoughts wandering spontaneously.

_____

F. I often allow my thoughts to wander on purpose.

_____

Once you've each answered all of the questions, it's time
to compute a few measures of your personality:

Sustained Interest Score: 20 − (A + C) = ____
Sustained Effort Score: B + D = ____
Grit Score: Sustained Interest + Sustained Effort = ____

The hypothesis

The higher your answer to question E, the lower your Grit Score
(as defined in the Research section) is expected to be. And the
higher your answer to question F, the higher your Sustained
Effort Score is expected to be.

The research

When our minds wander from a task that requires sustained

interest and attention, it stands to reason that we are likely to miss important information or perform the task poorly or inefficiently. But a 2017 study found that whether mind-wandering is intentional makes a big difference in terms of its association with grit, a personality trait that an influential 2007 study described as encompassing two other traits: sustained interest in projects or activities and sustained effort in the face of obstacles.

As part of the 2017 study, participants were asked to answer questions about their level of sustained interest in activities or projects; their tenacity in the face of obstacles; and their propensity for both spontaneous and deliberate mind-wandering. When the researchers examined the responses, they found that higher values for spontaneous mind-wandering were associated with lower scores related to grit. The same was not true for deliberate mind-wandering. Higher values for deliberate mind-wandering had a mild association with a greater perseverance of effort, although they did not appear to have any significant relationship with sustained interest.

Why would spontaneous mind-wandering be different from deliberate mind-wandering, in terms of its association with gritty behavior? One explanation is that deliberate mind-wandering involves resource prioritization, in which we momentarily direct our attention away from lower-priority goals to attend to higher-priority goals, and that behavior may ultimately help, rather than hurt, our chances of achieving our highest-priority goals.

The researchers note, however, that it's premature to say which factor causes which. Perhaps grit, as a personality trait, causes less spontaneous mind-wandering. Or maybe less spontaneous mind-wandering enables the completion of short-term and longer-term goals, and out of that pattern of successful behavior the personality trait of grit develops.

(!) The takeaway

Your own individual Grit Score and its relationship to mind-wandering may help you learn something about your own personality and behaviors, but perhaps more important is how your results line up with those of your spouse. Is there a mismatch in your scores, with one spouse high and one spouse low? That's something to be mindful of as a couple, because it might present challenges related to your motivations, shared expectations, and ability to follow through with commitments. Do both of you have high Grit Scores? That bodes well for your marriage. High grit is associated with a decreased likelihood of divorce (at least in men), probably because grit involves remaining committed to goals even in the face of challenges, and divorce often happens when the challenges facing a marriage seem insurmountable. Do both of you have low Grit Scores? If so, be each other's support system, encouraging your spouse to persevere when times get rough and to finish uncompleted projects.

Research Areas: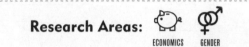

ECONOMICS   GENDER DIFFERENCES

The experiment

For this experiment, you should each imagine that you have been given the opportunity to earn money in a series of lottery drawings. In all nine hypothetical lotteries, you will be presented with two options, each of which has its own payout structure. For each case, both of you should write down on separate sheets

of paper whether you would prefer to participate in Lottery A or Lottery B.

Lottery A

1. 10% chance of $100,
   90% chance of $80
2. 20% chance of $100,
   80% chance of $80
3. 30% chance of $100,
   70% chance of $80
4. 40% chance of $100,
   60% chance of $80
5. 50% chance of $100,
   50% chance of $80
6. 60% chance of $100,
   40% chance of $80
7. 70% chance of $100,
   30% chance of $80
8. 80% chance of $100,
   20% chance of $80
9. 90% chance of $100,
   10% chance of $80

Lottery B

1. 10% chance of $190,
   90% chance of $5
2. 20% chance of $190,
   80% chance of $5
3. 30% chance of $190,
   70% chance of $5
4. 40% chance of $190,
   60% chance of $5
5. 50% chance of $190,
   50% chance of $5
6. 60% chance of $190,
   40% chance of $5
7. 70% chance of $190,
   30% chance of $5
8. 80% chance of $190,
   20% chance of $5
9. 90% chance of $190,
   10% chance of $5

🕐 The hypothesis

Whether you are a man or a woman, you are likely to have chosen Lottery B about the same amount of times. If there is a difference in your tallies, men are more likely than women to have shown a greater preference for Lottery B, but the difference is probably slight.

🔬 The research

The experiment you just performed was adapted from an influential 2002 study on risk aversion, which has been replicated hundreds of times since then. Researchers in a 2016 study gathered data from dozens of such replications that included data on the genders of the participants to further examine the claim that women are more risk-averse than men. Although a variety of research has found supporting evidence of the claim, the 2016 study's authors noted that a large data set focused on a single task—in this case, choosing between sets of lottery options—would increase statistical power and be the best means to gauge the true magnitude of the effect. What they found was that on this particular task, the difference between women's and men's choices was very slight. Men did choose the riskier lottery option more, but only by one-sixth of a standard deviation, which the authors describe as "economically unimportant."

Why would other previous research have found a gender disparity of a much higher magnitude? The authors think that gender differences are highly dependent on the way the experiment is designed, and if you design the experiment correctly, you can all but eliminate the difference in risk profiles between the genders. In particular, they suggest that gender differences are more likely to be found when an experiment includes a risk-free option and when it is the payoff amounts, rather than the probabilities, that vary. The experiment you performed does not include a risk-free option, since you always have at least a 10 percent chance of receiving the lower amount, and it keeps the payoff amounts consistent but varies the probabilities. Thus, according to the study, this type of task is likely to result in a relatively small gender difference.

ⓘ The takeaway

The seemingly wide agreement in academic literature that women are more risk-averse than men also seeps into everyday life. You're probably familiar with a stereotype applied to women in which they value security and stability above all else, and an opposing stereotype applied to men in which they are painted as brash adventure seekers who thrive in high-risk scenarios. It turns out those stereotypes may not have much truth to them. If, at least in certain scenarios, men and women have essentially the same level of risk aversion, then in scenarios where a gender difference is detected, it may have more to do with the particulars of the task than with underlying attitudes about risk. In your own marriage, it's entirely possible that the two of you have different levels of risk aversion, but the results of this study suggest that your risk profile may have more to do with your personality than your gender. Husbands, don't assume that your wife is necessarily more risk-averse, or that wives in general are more risk-averse than husbands in general. And wives, don't assume the converse. If you do, the risk you're taking is letting your thinking be guided by stereotypes rather than evidence.

27
FUTURE DISCOUNT

Research Areas:

DECISION   ECONOMICS
MAKING

 **The experiment**

In this experiment, five scenarios will be described. You should first each consider the scenarios individually, without discussing them with your partner, and write down your answers on separate sheets of paper. Then, you should repeat the process, but this time discussing the scenarios as a couple and making joint decisions.

Imagine that you get to choose between two prizes. In each of the five scenarios, Prize A is $1,200, but you have to wait a certain amount of time before receiving it. Prize B is an unknown amount of money, but you only have to wait a week to receive it. Your job is to determine the lowest value of Prize B that would make you prefer it to Prize A. For example, if you have to wait two weeks to receive Prize A, but you only have to wait one week to receive Prize B, you might say that you would be willing to accept $1,150 as Prize B rather than waiting the additional week to get the full $1,200.

For each of the following five scenarios, write down the lowest monetary value of Prize B for which you would still prefer it to Prize A:

Wait one month to receive Prize A, but only one week to receive Prize B.

Wait three months to receive Prize A, but only one week to receive Prize B.

Wait six months to receive Prize A, but only one week to receive Prize B.

Wait one year to receive Prize A, but only one week to receive Prize B.

Wait two years to receive Prize A, but only one week to receive Prize B.

Remember, once you have each individually written down your answers to the five scenarios, you should discuss the scenarios as a couple and jointly make the decisions.

🔮 The hypothesis

The values you assign to Prize B as a couple will be higher than the values that either of you assigned to Prize B individually.

🔬 The research

In a 2013 study about how individuals and couples differ in their decision-making, participants (who were all romantic couples who had been living together for at least a year) were first interviewed individually and asked to respond to scenarios like the ones described on the previous page. They were then brought together as a couple and prompted to make joint decisions about the same scenarios.

The researchers found that across the scenarios, the median responses from couples were higher than the median responses from men or women individually. For example, when the waiting period for Prize B was a week and the waiting period for Prize A was two years, women were willing to accept a prize amount for Prize B that was 71 percent of the prize amount for Prize A. Men were willing to accept a discount of 76 percent. But for couples, the discount was 80 percent. This suggests that couples weren't using compromise strategies, in which they arrive at some mutually agreeable value that lies in between their individual choices. Instead, the act of making joint decisions appears to increase the couple's tolerance for time delays.

(ⓘ) The takeaway

For researchers, the clear takeaway is that using the preferences or behavior of one member of a married couple to represent or model the preferences or behavior of the couple is going to lead to inaccuracies. In fact, researchers can't even survey both of the members and average their responses. Instead, to ensure accuracy, they have to interview the couple together and allow them to make truly joint decisions.

For married couples, one practical takeaway is that there are going to be some circumstances in which your joint decisions are not going to fall in the midrange between your individual preferences. Assuming you don't know with certainty which circumstances those are, it calls into question whether you can ever confidently infer your joint preferences—even if you already know your partner's individual preferences. The best way, then, to make mutually satisfying decisions as a couple is to actually discuss and deliberate as a couple. If you find yourself in a situation where you must make a decision that affects both you and your spouse, rather than trying to assume you can make the decision on behalf of both of you, let your default response be, "We'll have to discuss it together."

PART 5

WRITE IT OUT

28

GOOD, BAD, AND BETTER THAN OTHERS

Research Areas: 👁 💎

PERCEPTION   RELATIONSHIP
QUALITY

🧪 The experiment

Both of you will need a pen and paper handy for this one. You'll briefly answer the same two questions about relationships and partners, but before you get to the questions, flip a coin to determine who should follow Instructions A and who should follow Instructions B. The spouse who will be following Instructions A should turn to page 248 to read them and answer the questions. The other spouse should turn to page 256 to read their instructions and answer the questions.

❓ The hypothesis

You will each have placed check marks next to more than 50 percent of the good features you listed in response to Question

1 and fewer than 50 percent of the bad features you listed in response to Question 2. But the spouse who read Instructions B is likely to have a higher number of check marks for Question 1 and a lower number of check marks for Question 2 than the spouse who read Instructions A.

The research

In a 2000 study involving young adults in established romantic relationships, researchers examined whether the participants regarded their own relationship as having more good qualities and fewer bad qualities than other people's relationships. The researchers were also curious whether the participants' responses might be influenced by instructions that were intended to heighten or dampen this "perceived superiority" effect.

They posed questions similar to Question 1 and Question 2 to several groups of people, with each group receiving a different set of instructions beforehand. One group, dubbed the "threat" group, received instructions that emphasized that young adults' relationships are less likely than other types of relationships to endure. The researchers suspected that by introducing doubt about the durability of participants' relationships, it would cause the participants to lean heavily on perceived superiority as a way

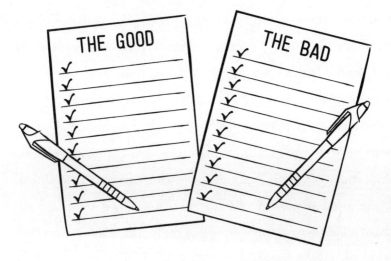

of reassuring themselves that their own relationships weren't in trouble. Another group, dubbed the "accuracy" group, received instructions that encouraged them to be as accurate and honest as possible in their responses. The researchers suspected that if the instructions emphasized the need for honest evaluation, the participants would be less likely to view their own relationships through rose-colored glasses.

The results showed that the perceived superiority effect was indeed present. The participants were more likely to associate their own relationships and partners with the good features, and other people's relationships and partners with the bad features.

And as the researchers suspected, the "threat" and "accuracy" groups did respond differently. Among participants who scored highly on a pretest designed to measure their level of relationship commitment, those in the "accuracy" group listed an average of eight good features and identified about 80 percent of them as features more typical of their own relationships than of others' relationships. But those in the "threat" group listed an average of ten good features and identified just about all of them as more typical of their own relationships than of others' relationships.

These results support the idea that perceived superiority is a real phenomenon in relationships, and that it can be either heightened or dampened. But why does it exist at all, and what value does it offer? The study's authors gave a few potential explanations. For instance, it might help couples cope when their relationship is going through a rough patch. Thinking positively about your relationship during these periods might make it more likely for you to weather the storm and end up with a positive outcome. Perceived superiority might also help couples maintain confidence in their relationship in the face of doubts (such as gloomy statistics about divorce rates). Even if that confidence is actually overconfidence and our perception of our partner is idealized rather than strictly accurate, previous research has shown that it can nevertheless contribute to a feeling of satisfaction in the relationship.

(!) The takeaway

Newlyweds tend to be both highly committed to and highly satisfied with their relationships. Over the long haul, however, you will inevitably face difficulties that can threaten both your level of commitment and your level of satisfaction. As with life in general, having optimistic expectations about your relationship's future can actually influence the success of your marriage, and the perceived superiority effect is one way that we might generate those optimistic expectations, even if they're slightly biased in our favor. You might try to reinforce this positive attitude within your own relationship by periodically making lists of the good, the bad, and the things that make your relationship better than the rest.

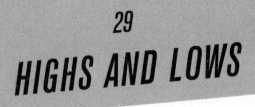

29
HIGHS AND LOWS

Research Areas: CONSTRUAL   SELF CONTROL

 **The experiment**

There are two parts to this project. For the first part, flip a coin to determine who will be in the "Why" condition and who will be in the "How" condition. The "Why" spouse should turn to page 248 for instructions. The "How" spouse should turn to page 257 for instructions.

In the second part of the project, imagine you're at a silent auction. Each of you should jot down how much you would be willing to bid for the following items:

A four-pack of movie tickets at your favorite theater, which can be used immediately.

A four-pack of movie tickets at your favorite theater,
   which can't be used until six months from now.

A $100 gift card to your favorite restaurant, which can
   be used immediately.

A $100 gift card to your favorite restaurant,
   which can't be used until six months
   from now.

 A $50 gift card to your favorite bookstore,
   which can be used immediately.

A $50 gift card to your favorite bookstore, which can't
   be used until one year from now.

The hypothesis

Both of you are likely to bid lower for the items with delayed avail-
ability than for the immediately available items. But when you look
at the difference between what you bid for the two types of items,
there will be a more pronounced difference in bids by the spouse
in the "How" condition than by the spouse in the "Why" condition.

The research

There are a lot of ways to conceptualize self-control. You might
think about it as the ability to suppress instinctive behaviors, or the

ability to act in accordance with long-term goals rather than short-term goals, or the ability to act rationally rather than emotionally.

Researchers in a 2006 study wanted to explore another way to conceptualize self-control. They point out that there is often more than one way to interpret a particular situation. Higher-level interpretations of a situation are more abstract and more generalized, and they focus on primary features. Lower-level interpretations are more concrete and more specific, and they may focus on secondary features. For instance, you might look at a landscape painting and say, "There are a bunch of individual trees." Or you might interpret the scene at a higher level and say, "That's a forest!"

The study's authors describe self-control as the ability to act in accordance with the higher-level interpretation rather than the lower-level interpretation of a situation. For instance, when you're offered some junk food, a higher-level interpretation might be, "I'm trying to lose weight, and this treat won't help me reach that goal," while a lower-level interpretation might be, "Boy, I'm hungry, and this treat looks delicious!" The authors wanted to investigate whether helping a person interpret a situation in higher-level terms might help them exert self-control.

To test this theory, they devised an experiment in which

some participants were primed to think in terms of higher-level interpretations (the "Why" condition) and others were primed to think in terms of lower-level interpretations (the "How" condition). The participants were then presented with a list of items that they could receive either immediately or at some point in the future and were asked to identify how much they would be willing to pay for those items.

The researchers expected that all of the participants, regardless of which group they were in, would value the delayed-availability items less than the immediately available items. But if their theory were correct and higher-level interpretations are associated with an increase in self-control, then the participants who had been primed to think in terms of lower-level interpretations would value delayed-availability items far less than the immediately available items, because they would be less able to exercise the self-control needed to wait for the item. On the other hand, the participants who had been primed to think in terms of higher-level interpretations would not be expected to have such a large spread between how they valued the items, because they would be better able to exercise the self-control needed to wait for the item.

It turns out that the people in the "How" group did, indeed, place a much higher value on the immediately available items than on the delayed-availability items, compared with those in the "Why" group. The "How" group bid, on average, about $30 for the immediately available movie tickets but about $21.50 for the delayed-availability tickets. To put it another way, the delayed-availability tickets were seen as only about 72 percent as valuable as the immediately available tickets. The "Why" group, on the other hand, bid about $28.50 for the immediately available tickets and about $24.50 for the delayed-availability tickets. Thus, the delayed-availability tickets were seen as 86 percent as valuable. These results provide support for the idea that how we interpret a particular situation can influence the level of self-control we exert. Being willing to wait for delayed gratification is, after all, a hallmark of self-control.

ⓘ The takeaway

You and your spouse are likely to face plenty of occasions when exercising self-control is necessary. To maintain your weight or health, you might need to pass on a delectable dessert. To keep your budget in check, you might have to put off a wardrobe update. To keep the peace when houseguests overstay their welcome, you might have to bite your tongue.

One way to steer yourself and your spouse toward higher-level interpretations, which might help you practice self-control, is to put some sort of distance between you and the objects of your decisions. That might be physical distance, such as storing candy in a hard-to-reach place rather than within arm's reach; social distance, such as thinking about the situation in terms of how you would advise another person to act, rather than how you yourself would like to act; or temporal distance, such as by putting off an emotionally charged decision so you and your spouse can take more time to think it through.

30

TABOO MEMORY AID

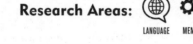

Research Areas:

LANGUAGE   MEMORY

 **The experiment**

You'll each get a chance to conduct a version of this experiment on your spouse. Flip a coin to decide who will play the role of Experimenter first. The Experimenter should grab a sheet of paper and write down five emotionally neutral words (e.g., "attic" or "shoebox"), five emotionally charged words (e.g., "hate" or "adore"), and five taboo words (e.g., profanities or slurs).

Now the Experimenter should point to each word in a random order, and your spouse should indicate with a thumbs-up or thumbs-down whether each word begins with a vowel. Check off each word as it is used.

After this, take ten minutes to engage in some other activity that involves mental work, such as completing a crossword puzzle together or playing a video game. Next, the spouse should try to recall the fifteen words that were on the list.

Now it's time to switch roles. Again, the spouse in the Experimenter role should come up with a list of five emotionally neutral words, five emotionally charged words, and five taboo words.

This time, the Experimenter should recite their list of words in a random order, and their spouse should indicate with a thumbs-up or thumbs-down whether each word could fit into the sentence: *The _____ is blue.*

After this, take another ten minutes to engage in an activity that involves mental work. Then the spouse should try to recall the fifteen words on the list.

⑦ The hypothesis

The spouse who identified which words began with a vowel will be able to recall fewer neutral words than the spouse who identified which words fit into the sentence. Both spouses will do slightly better at recalling the emotionally charged words and significantly better at recalling the taboo words.

 **The research**

Participants in a 2008 study were shown a list of words from three categories (neutral, emotional, and taboo) and were asked a question about each word that required them to process the word at either a shallow, visual level ("Does the word begin with a vowel?") or at a deeper, semantic level ("Does the word fit into a given sentence?").

Then, after an unrelated mental task, they were asked to recall all of the words. As anticipated, the participants were able to recall slightly more emotional words than neutral words, and significantly more taboo words than neutral words. The researchers think this occurs because words with emotional content arouse our attention, and words with taboo content do so even more.

The study also found that when a deep processing task was used, the participants recalled more neutral words than when a shallow processing task was used. But that didn't hold true for the emotional or taboo words. Based on those results, the researchers concluded that deep processing may help arouse our attention, but if our attention is already aroused because of the nature of the words themselves, then it has little additional effect.

(!) The takeaway

Memory is a tricky thing. What makes us remember some things but easily forget others? The results of this study point to a couple of factors that can make a memory stickier: processing memory items on a deep level, and the attention-arousing content of the items. So, when your spouse has forgotten to fold the laundry yet again, perhaps some choice words might serve as a memory aid.

31
JOTTING THANKS

Research Area:

EMOTIONS

 **The experiment**

In this experiment, each of you will complete a weekly question-naire over a three-week period. Additionally, one of you will be given an extra assignment. Flip a coin to determine which spouse gets the extra assignment.

Once a week (beginning today) and continuing for the next three weeks, each of you should record your answers to the following statements, using a scale from 1 (strongly disagree) to 10 (strongly agree):

I feel satisfied with my life. ____

Compared to my peers, I consider myself a very
happy person. ____

I tend to enjoy life, regardless of what's going on. ____

In most ways, my life is close to my ideal. ____

In this past week, I felt bothered by things that don't

   usually bother me. ____

I have so much in my life to feel thankful for. ____

The spouse who gets the extra assignment should turn to page 249 to read instructions about the assignment.

🔎 The hypothesis

When you compare the values of your questionnaires across the course of the experiment, the spouse who completed the extra assignment is likely to see an increase in values, while the other spouse's values are likely to remain roughly steady.

🔬 The research

The authors of a 2012 study about how gratitude affects well-being split participants into two groups. Those in the experiment group wrote letters of gratitude over a three-week period, while those in the control group did not. Both before and after the letter writing, all participants completed questionnaires that measured various aspects of well-being, such as happiness,

gratitude, depressive symptoms, and life
satisfaction. The researchers found
that the participants who wrote
letters of gratitude reported greater
feelings of happiness and life satisfaction,
and fewer depressive symptoms, than they did before the letter
writing started, whereas the values remained flat for participants in the control condition. Surprisingly, the only measure
of well-being that didn't benefit from writing letters of gratitude
was gratitude itself. The researchers speculated, based on these
findings, that our level of gratitude may be more of a fixed aspect
of our personality, and so not as susceptible to influence by letter
writing as our level of happiness or other measures of mood.

The takeaway

Perhaps one of the first joint projects that most newlyweds
undertake once they've settled in after their wedding is the
task of writing thank-you notes to their guests, well-wishers,

and gift-givers. Whether you are writing just
a few notes of thanks or hundreds, be sure to
take the time to let the recipients know not
only that you appreciate any gift they might

have given, but also that you are grateful for their love, support, and friendship. It's a great way to strengthen and maintain your bonds with your loved ones—and, as a bonus, the results of this study suggest that expressing your gratitude will lift your own spirits as well!

GRATEFUL, AND FEELING GREAT

The benefits of a grateful disposition go well beyond the pick-me-up you feel when you write a letter of gratitude. A 2009 study found, for instance, that a sense of gratitude is associated with a greater perception that life is both manageable and meaningful. A 2010 study found that expressing gratitude to one's partner is associated with an increased perception of the strength of the relationship. And outside of romantic partnerships, gratitude has the potential to help build everyday relationships, a 2012 study found, by promoting social behaviors, such as wishing to spend time with a benefactor.

32
MALLEABLE ME

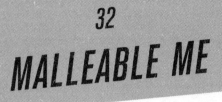

Research Areas: **MOTIVATION** **SELF ESTEEM**

 The experiment

You and your spouse will each need a sheet of writing paper and a pen. For the first part of the project, you should separately try to recall a recent time when you did something you knew was wrong and that led to feelings of guilt and remorse. The transgression should be something that still makes you feel bad when you think about it. Write down a few sentences on your own sheet of paper describing this incident.

For the second part of the project, flip a coin to determine who will read Instructions A on page 249 and who will read Instructions B on page 257.

Once you have completed the second part, each of you

should answer the following prompts on a scale from 1 (not at all true) to 10 (very true):

> I am committed to not repeating this behavior again.
>
> ____
>
> Realistically, it's likely that I'll do something like this again in the future. ____
>
> I feel no need to make amends. ____
>
> If I try hard enough, I will be successful at avoiding this behavior. ____

🧠 The hypothesis

The spouse who read Instructions A is more likely than the spouse who read Instructions B to express a desire to make amends and a firm commitment to avoid the behavior in the future.

🔬 The research

In a 2012 study on ways to increase motivation for self-improvement, participants were asked to recall a moral transgression and to write a self-addressed note focused either on self-compassion (recognizing that we all make mistakes and responding with warmth and understanding) or self-esteem (reminding oneself of one's good qualities). The participants were then asked questions about how committed they were to making amends, changing the behavior, and avoiding temptation in the future.

The study's authors found that the people in the self-compassion condition were more likely than those in the self-esteem condition to view the behavior as changeable, to express a desire to change and make amends, and to feel confident that they will successfully avoid the behavior in the future.

In related experiments, participants in the self-compassion condition were also found to be more motivated to improve not only in regard to moral behaviors, but also in regard to personal weaknesses and academic failures. That's intriguing, because typically both self-compassion and self-esteem are considered positive measures of well-being. Yet in the context of self-improvement, it appears that self-compassion has an edge, possibly because focusing on self-esteem might lead to an inflated self-appraisal and an attitude that fails to recognize that improvement is needed, whereas focusing on self-compassion encourages a realistic, nonjudgmental self-appraisal that doesn't brush over the weakness but also doesn't blow it out of proportion.

⊞ The takeaway

You and your spouse will likely struggle at times with personal weaknesses, moral failings, and failures to achieve certain goals. Your attitude toward these problems can help influence your motivation to improve. You might think that a focus on self-compassion might lead you to be too easy on yourself, fail to set high enough standards for yourself, or fail to follow through with efforts to improve. But the results of this study suggest that the benefits of a self-compassionate approach don't hurt improvement efforts and can actually help them. As you confront the areas of your own life where you fall short, try to adopt a self-compassionate mindset. And when your spouse is dealing with a personal failing or weakness in a way that is highly self-critical or despairing, your expressions of empathy and understanding might help kindle in them an attitude of self-compassion, which, combined with your support, can work wonders.

33
MIND-MELD MEMORIES

🧪 The experiment

For this exercise, you'll need to agree on a movie to watch that neither of you has seen before. After watching, agree on a scene that involved a lot of detail—fast action, rich dialogue, vivid scenery—and separately write down everything you remember about that scene: what the characters said and did, what they were wearing, what was around them, etc. Then get together and

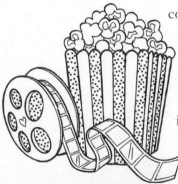

compare notes. When possible, repeat, rephrase, or elaborate on each other's recollections. Finally, re-watch your chosen scene and note what you individually and collaboratively got right and wrong about the scene.

❓ The hypothesis

Although collaborating with your spouse might not enable you to recall significantly more, it will help you reduce errors you may have made in your individual recollections.

🔬 The research

Research has shown that when two people collaboratively recall an event, one person's memories can influence those of the other person. For instance, a 2006 study found that the person who initiates the discussion about an event detail is more likely to influence the other person than the other way around. In certain situations, this "memory conformity" effect can have very serious consequences. For example, witnesses to a crime who have discussed the event together might appear to be corroborating each other's memories, when in fact one person's version of the event has unduly influenced the other's.

But not all shared recollections are equally sensitive to that effect. A 2014 study found romantic couples were not particularly susceptible to the negative effects of collaborative recall, and in fact couples in strong, intimate relationships were able to recall more together than either individual could alone.

A 2015 study set out to determine whether collaborative

recall might have another upside. Participants attended a play and were later asked to recall details about a particularly emotional three-minute scene. Some of the participants were interviewed only individually about the scene, while others were couples who were interviewed both individually and then together as a couple. The researchers found that both groups recalled roughly the same number of accurate details about the scene, but the couples in the collaborative condition made fewer errors. They also found that couples who used active listening strategies, such as repeating, rephrasing, or elaborating upon each other's recollections, were able to recall more facts about the scene.

(!) The takeaway

Recalling shared memories, such as a luxurious vacation or a night out with close friends, can be a pleasurable way for a couple to pass the time, and in many cases the accuracy or inaccuracy of those memories has little consequence. But sometimes the details matter, and it's nice to know that collaborating with your spouse to recall an event can help reduce the number of false memories you report. The results of this research show, however, that the manner in which you communicate during your discussions has an effect on the quality of your recollections. And the active listening style, in which you indicate that you've understood your partner's words by repeating them or rephrasing them, can not only help with memory recall but also with communication in general. So whether you're trying to remember the details of your first date, or just listening to your spouse talk about something that happened today, be sure to give your full attention and demonstrate that you're focused on what they are saying. It'll make for more happy memories down the line.

34

THE POWER OF US

Research Areas: CONFLICT RESOLUTION • EMOTIONS • SOCIAL PSYCHOLOGY

The experiment

There are four stages to this experiment. Your task in the first stage is to work together to come up with three sources of conflict in your relationship. They don't need to be issues that are causing conflict right at this moment—it's sufficient that they have come up in your relationship at some point in the past and are likely to be the source of future conflict.

The second stage pertains to conflict resolution when one member of a couple is in charge, so flip a coin to determine who will serve as the Leader and who will serve as the Follower. The Leader should select one of the three topics to discuss further. Leader, for five minutes, you should guide the conversation however you see fit, working with your spouse to try to resolve this source of conflict. Follower, you should follow the lead of your spouse, being careful to observe the Leader-Follower dynamic.

In the third stage, each of you should individually complete the following exercise. Observe the four payout scales below. Imagine that you and an acquaintance will each receive one payout from each scale, and that you get to decide which payout it will be. Select one column (labeled A through D) from each of the four scales.

PAYOUT SCALE #1	A	B	C	D
YOU GET:	$50	$65	$70	$75
THEY GET:	$100	$90	$80	$70

PAYOUT SCALE #2	A	B	C	D
YOU GET:	$50	$60	$70	$80
THEY GET:	$100	$80	$50	$30

PAYOUT SCALE #3	A	B	C	D
YOU GET:	$100	$85	$60	$50
THEY GET:	$50	$60	$85	$100

PAYOUT SCALE #4	A	B	C	D
YOU GET:	$100	$95	$90	$85
THEY GET:	$50	$60	$70	$85

In the fourth stage, each of you should individually write down the degree to which you felt the following emotions during your conflict resolution discussion and the degree to which you think your partner felt the emotions. For each, use a scale from 1 (very low) to 10 (very high):

Angry	I felt: _____	My spouse felt: _____
Appreciated	I felt: _____	My spouse felt: _____
Caring	I felt: _____	My spouse felt: _____
Confident	I felt: _____	My spouse felt: _____
Insecure	I felt: _____	My spouse felt: _____
Sad	I felt: _____	My spouse felt: _____

The hypothesis

For the spouse who was designated the Leader, the accuracy of your guesses about the degree to which your partner felt the six listed emotions will be associated with your choices in the payoff scales. The more accurate your guesses, the more likely it is that you chose payoffs that maximized joint reward, possibly at the expense of yourself. The less accurate your guesses, the more likely it is that you chose payoffs that maximized your own reward, possibly at the expense of the other person. For the spouse who was designated the Follower, things are a little different. If your spouse made payoff choices that maximized their own reward, you are likely to be more accurate overall at guessing your spouse's emotions, regardless of the payoff choices you made.

🔬 The research

Researchers in a 2013 study examined how a feeling of power within a romantic relationship is associated with understanding and considering the other partner's perspective during conflict resolution.

In one of the study's experiments, each member of a romantic couple was assigned to either a high-power condition, where they led and made choices during a conflict resolution task, or a low-power condition, where they followed their partner's lead and did not have the opportunity to make choices. Then they each engaged in an exercise similar to the payoff exercise you completed, which was designed to reveal whether the person primarily engages in pro-social behavior (behavior that maximizes joint rewards) or pro-self behavior (behavior that maximizes a person's own reward). Finally, they answered questions about their own emotions during the conflict resolution task, as well as questions about what they thought their partner's emotions were during the same task.

The researchers found that for participants who were primarily pro-self, being placed in the Leader position made their guesses about their partner's emotions less accurate. In contrast, for participants who were primarily pro-social, the accuracy of their guesses was about the same, regardless of whether they were in the Leader role or the Follower role.

The results suggest that among romantic partners who are more self-focused, having power in the relationship reduces their ability to consider their partner's perspective, but among those who are more other-focused, having power in the relationship enhances (or at least does not detract from) their ability to consider their partner's perspective. This was consistent with earlier results from a 2001 study that suggests that power tends to magnify the effect of whatever our natural inclinations might be.

(!) The takeaway

Robert G. Ingersoll, one of the most popular orators of the late 1800s, once said of Abraham Lincoln: "Nothing discloses real character like the use of power. It is easy for the weak to be gentle. Most people can bear adversity. But if you wish to know what a man really is, give him power. This is the supreme test. It is the glory of Lincoln that, having almost absolute power, he never abused it, except upon the side of mercy."

The results of this study seem to suggest that although power is a general magnifier of our character, the magnification is especially large when our deepest tendencies are oriented toward the self, rather than to others. If that applies to one or the both of you, you may need to make a concerted effort to ensure that a power imbalance in your relationship—whether it pertains to your finances, social clout, or some other factor—doesn't do you in. Try to make joint decisions about issues that affect both of you, consult your spouse even when the decision is primarily one that you are empowered to make, and consider your spouse's perspective when you can't ask them about it directly.

35

WHAT MIGHT HAVE BEEN

Research Areas:

PERSONALITY SOCIAL PSYCHOLOGY

🧪 The experiment

Flip a coin to determine who will be in the Factual condition and who will be in the Counterfactual condition. Each of you should select a close friend, such as one of your groomsmen or bridesmaids, who will serve as the subject of a writing prompt. The spouse who is in the Factual condition should refer to the writing prompt on page 250. The spouse who is in the Counterfactual condition should refer to the writing prompt on page 257.

The spouse who is in the Factual condition should refer to the writing prompt on page 250. The spouse who is in the Counterfactual condition should refer to the writing prompt on page 257.

Once you have both written about your close friends, you should individually answer the following three statements, using a scale from 1 (strongly disagree) to 10 (strongly agree):

My friendship with this person defines who I am. ____

My friendship with this person has added meaning to
my life. ____

Choosing this friendship has been among the most
significant choices in my life. ____

ⓘ The hypothesis

The spouse in the Counterfactual condition is likely to have given higher answers to the three statements above than the spouse in the Factual condition.

🔬 The research

Counterfactual thinking entails imagining what might have happened if things had not gone the way they actually did. The authors of a 2010 study were interested in whether engaging in this type of thinking might affect how people perceive the meaningfulness of a close relationship.

Participants were divided into two groups. The first group was asked to write an essay about how they met a close friend and how their friendship developed. The second group was asked to write an essay about how they could easily have not met this friend, and how their life might have been different as a result. Both groups were then prompted to rate how meaning-ful the friendship has been to their life. The researchers found that the group who engaged in counterfactual thinking ascribed more meaning to the friendship than the other group.

In a related experiment, the researchers found that counterfactual thinking not only led people to treat relationships or significant events as more meaningful but also made them more likely to describe them as fated or part of their destiny. This may seem surprising, since the whole point of counterfac-tual thinking is to reflect on how things could have easily turned out differently. The researchers think, however, that when subjects made the effort to consider how many variables had to line up just right to produce a particular outcome, they were more likely to view the outcome as improbable, and more likely to reason that since the outcome occurred despite the odds, it must have been "meant to be."

The takeaway

As you and your spouse think about your own "story of us," it might be worthwhile to consider how easily the encounter that led to your becoming a couple might have instead been a missed connection. What meaning do you ascribe to the fact that things unfolded the way they did, and that they continued to unfold, leading to your eventual "I do"? That's for you and your spouse to determine. Maybe it was fate, maybe it was mere coincidence, or maybe what really matters is that you're both on the same page about its meaning. However you view things, remember that just as there are many ways the past might have been different, there are also many ways the future could unfold, depending, in part, on your choices in the present. So choose wisely!

PART 6

CHECK IN OVER TIME

36

AW, I'M TOUCHED

Research Areas: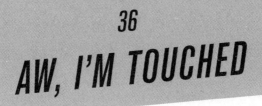

EMOTIONS RELATIONSHIP
QUALITY

 **The experiment**

For this project, both of you will need a notepad or a digital note-taking application. Over the course of a week, you will each periodically jot down small notes about your feelings and interactions.

Twice a day (once around midday and once before bed) for seven days, each of you should separately and privately take a couple of minutes to jot down your answers to the following prompts. For the first four statements, use a scale from 1 (strongly disagree) to 10 (strongly agree):

1. I feel physically, mentally, and emotionally well right now. ____

2. I feel content with my life right now. ____

3. I feel close to my spouse right now. ____

4. I feel well understood by my spouse right now. ____

5. Since the last report, about how many times have you hugged, caressed, affectionately touched, or held hands with your spouse? ____

At the end of the week, it's time for the two of you to crunch the data. In total, there should be fourteen entries in each of your notes. For each entry, tell your partner your response to Question 5 and allow them to write it alongside the corresponding entry in their notes.

The hypothesis

For entries in which affectionate touch occurred (either by you or your spouse), your answers to the other four questions should show a rise in value. The more instances of affectionate touch occurring, the larger the rise in value you should expect to see.

The research

Couples in a 2013 study were asked to keep a weeklong diary that tracked their mood, their feelings of intimacy with their partner, and their use of affectionate touch. The study's authors then examined the data to see whether the use of affectionate touch was associated with a rise in either mood or feelings of intimacy. They found that there was indeed a positive correlation. The more affectionate touch occurred, either by self or by spouse, the higher the observed rise was in the other data.

Beyond the immediate positive effects of affectionate touch, the researchers also found that it was associated with longer-lasting positive outcomes. Six months after the original study, the participants completed a follow-up survey intended to measure their psychological well-being. Those who had experienced a high amount of affectionate touch during the experiment period tended to have a higher level of well-being, based on their responses to the follow-up survey, than people who had experienced a low amount of affectionate touch.

(!) The takeaway

The benefits of touch are many. It lifts our moods and our feelings of intimacy with our spouse, and related research has demonstrated that it also has the ability to both lower stress and prevent stress responses from occurring.

For some couples, affectionate touch comes naturally.

Others might have to work at it. If you and your spouse aren't naturally touchy-feely, remember that even small gestures, such as holding hands, have the ability to let your spouse know that you're there for them. And remember, the study's results revealed that affectionate touch had a positive effect not just on the recipient, but on both people in the relationship. So even if affectionate touch comes more naturally to you than to your partner, or vice versa, both of you can expect to reap the benefits.

37

NOTICEABLE SUPPORT

Research Areas: 👁 ◇

PERCEPTION · RELATIONSHIP QUALITY

🧪 The experiment

Once each day for ten days straight, each of you should answer the following questions, but wait until the end to compare responses. Where ranges are specified, use a scale from 1 (very low) to 10 (very high):

> During the past day, did you share a negative event with your partner? (Y/N)
>
> How understanding was your partner's response? (1–10 or N/A)
>
> How valued did your partner's response make you feel? (1–10 or N/A)

During the past day, did your partner share a negative
    event with you? (Y/N)
How understanding was your response? (1–10 or N/A)
How valued did you make your partner feel? (1–10 or N/A)
How positive was your mood over the past day? (1–10)
How connected to your partner did you feel over the
    past day? (1–10)

At the end of the ten days, look over your responses
together. Identify the occasions when one of you reported receiving support in response to sharing a negative event and the other
reported providing it. Also make note of any times when one
of you reported receiving support but the other did not report
providing it, or any times when one of you reported providing
support but the other did not report receiving it.

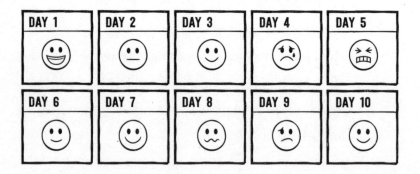

⑨ The hypothesis

Your mood and connectedness ratings are likely to have been lower when you perceived your spouse giving you support when you shared a negative event than when you did not perceive it but your partner reported offering it. Regardless of whether there was a match or a mismatch in your reported instances of support, however, the degree of responsiveness is likely to have been the biggest factor influencing your mood and connectedness ratings.

🔬 The research

Psychologists have observed in multiple studies about social support that merely receiving support isn't necessarily associated with better outcomes, such as an increase in positive mood or a stronger feeling of closeness to the person giving support. In fact, sometimes it can even lead to negative outcomes. There are a number of explanations for why that might be so. Maybe the person offering the support does so in a patronizing way. Maybe they don't have the right skills to properly support you, so they offer bad advice. Maybe the mere fact that support is being given is enough to lower your self-esteem.

Researchers in a 2008 study were curious about the difference between "visible" support, in which the person receiving the support was aware of receiving it, and "invisible" support, in which the person was not aware of receiving it. A previous study had suggested that invisible support might be more beneficial than visible support because when a person is aware of being a recipient of support, it might come with an emotional cost. For instance, a person might experience negative emotions, such as anxiety or depression, when they are aware of receiving support because it makes them feel more aware of the circumstances that led to the support being given.

But is a person's awareness of receiving support really what causes those negative outcomes?

The 2008 researchers thought there might be a more nuanced explanation. They had couples fill out a question-naire similar to the one at the beginning of this experiment and analyzed the various types of visible and invisible support the couples reported.

Consistent with the previous research, they found that when a person was aware of having received support, they reported greater sadness and anxiety and lower connectedness levels than when they were not aware of having received support, but their partner had reported offering support.

But then the researchers dug deeper and classified answers

by responsiveness—the degree to which the support can be characterized as understanding and respectful—and they found that in cases of visible support, a high degree of responsiveness was associated with neutral or positive outcomes, and in cases of invisible support, a low degree of responsiveness was associated with negative outcomes.

This suggests that while visibility versus invisibility does seem to have some effect on mood and relationship connectedness, it's really the quality of the partner's support that makes the biggest difference.

(‼) The takeaway

Your partner has had a bad day. Maybe work was especially aggravating, or they got a parking ticket, or a dear friend received a scary diagnosis. Your spouse comes home and wants to tell you about it. That's totally natural, and it's also natural for your spouse to expect you to be supportive. But, paradoxically, your partner's awareness of receiving support from you may have a hidden cost, at least if it's not done right.

Here's how to be the kind of highly responsive spouse who can offer effective support in times of trouble. First, be an attentive listener. Listening while multitasking is not ideal, and listening while keeping one eye on the game is pretty bad. Second, remember that your partner didn't share this information with you because they wanted a lecture. So even if you think your partner made some missteps that may have contributed to their negative experience, now is not the time to bring that up. Right now, what they're asking from you is genuine support. Make your spouse feel valued. Show that you understand and empathize with their sadness or frustration. Offer advice only if it's asked for, and only if you're qualified to give it. And even if you struggle to find words of consolation, a hug can go a long way toward helping your spouse feel genuinely supported.

38

TRAVEL TIME

Research Areas:

COMMUNICATION   EMOTIONS

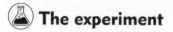

The experiment

You can conduct this experiment the next time one spouse needs to travel for more than a day without the other spouse, as on a business trip or a solitary visit to out-of-town relatives or friends. You should each keep a small daily logbook for the two days prior to the trip; each day of the trip itself; and the two days after the spouse who was traveling returns home. At the end of each day, rate the following statements in your logbook, using a scale of 1 (strongly disagree) to 10 (strongly agree):

My mood is positive, upbeat, and cheerful. ____
I am feeling extremely stressed. ____

I am experiencing physical discomfort (headache, knot

    in stomach, etc.) _____

I slept well last night. _____

I had pleasant interactions with my spouse today. _____

My spouse and I communicated frequently today. _____

A lot of good things happened to me today. _____

After you've completed your logbooks for the trip, as well as the two days before and after the trip, get together and compare your notes.

❓ The hypothesis

The spouse who stays at home is more likely to experience a dip in mood during the trip than the spouse who is traveling. Your mood is even more likely to dip if you're experiencing high anxiety. Frequent communication is likely to mitigate that dip. Both partners are likely to report more sleeping problems during the separation than before or afterward. But for most people, physical symptoms are likely to be the highest prior to the separation, then decline during the trip and either level out or decline further upon reunion.

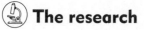 **The research**

A 2008 study looked at romantic partners who experience a brief separation when one of the partners must travel. Among the couples who participated in the study, the separation typically lasted between four and seven days. Each couple kept journals before, during, and after the trip, in which they responded to questions about their mood, stress levels, sleeping problems, and physical symptoms.

The study found that both the spouse who stayed at home and the spouse who was away experienced changes to mood and quality of sleep during the absence. Partners who remained at home reported high anxiety levels; those who had relatively brief contact with their traveling spouse experienced the largest negative change in mood. On the other end of the spectrum, traveling partners who were on pleasure trips, rather than business trips, experienced the least negative change in mood. Sleeping problems affected both partners, and high anxiety levels, particularly for the spouse who remained at home, exacerbated those sleeping problems, not only for the highly anxious spouse, but also for their partner. Contrary to the researchers' expectations, physical symptoms, such as headaches, did not increase once the separation commenced;

COMMUNICATION

rather, they were highest prior to the separation and then went down during the trip. Their explanation for those unexpected results is that the symptoms may be an unconscious way of signaling stress or anxiety to their spouse prior to departure, but once the spouse is gone, their signaling potential is lost, and they dissipate.

The results of the study, taken as a whole, show that separation due to travel can have a wide range of effects on both partners. A 2017 study examined whether there's anything travelers can do to reduce the negative effects of separation. It found that travelers who engage in preventive coping strategies—that is, figuring out in advance how to effectively cope with anticipated stressors, rather than waiting until those stressors are upon you—reported less emotional exhaustion, a greater feeling of work-life balance, and higher relationship satisfaction.

(I) The takeaway

Physical separation from the one you love, even if it's brief, and even if you've dealt with frequent travel before, can take a toll on both the partner who remains home and the partner who's away. Depending on your personalities, other stressors in your lives, and the degree to which you are able to communicate with each other during the absence, it might be felt as a minor disturbance or a significant upheaval. To reduce the stress the trip takes on both of you, plan ahead. If possible, arrange to talk on the phone or by video chat; hearing your spouse's voice can be incredibly comforting when they're miles away. Try to also stay in touch through email or text messages. If even written communication during the trip is difficult to arrange, perhaps you might write a love note or two that you can leave at home for your spouse to discover. And once the trip is over, make plans to spend some quality time together and celebrate the reunion.

39

CONFLICTS AND CUDDLING

Research Areas:

AFFECTION CONFLICT
RESOLUTION

🧪 The experiment

Every three days over the course of three weeks, you and your spouse should record your answer to the following question: On a scale from 1 (very easy) to 10 (very difficult), how difficult has it been to resolve conflicts with your spouse?

During that same three-week period, you and your spouse should make an effort to cuddle more frequently, and for a longer duration, than you usually do. For instance, if you usually cuddle for fifteen minutes, try to instead cuddle for twenty-five minutes. And if you usually cuddle two or three times a week, try to cuddle nearly every day instead.

The hypothesis

Over the course of the three weeks of extra cuddling, you and your spouse will report that conflict resolution is less difficult. You may also notice that other forms of intimate contact, such as kissing, have increased as well.

The research

Participants in a 2003 study reported how frequently they and their romantic partners engaged in several types of physical affection, such as kissing, hugging, and cuddling. They also completed a questionnaire about relationship satisfaction and conflict resolution. The results of the study showed that when couples engaged in these types of physical affection frequently, relationship satisfaction was higher, and conflict resolution was found to be easier.

A 2017 study looked at how cuddling, specifically, influences the health of a romantic relationship. Participants were divided into three groups. The first group was told to increase the frequency and duration of their cuddling. The second was told to increase the frequency and duration of shared meals. The third group was told not to do anything differently. The participants completed questionnaires about various aspects of their relationship over a multi-week period. The study found that those in the cuddling condition reported higher increases in relationship satisfaction and feelings of commitment compared with those in the shared-meals and control conditions. In both the cuddling and shared-meals conditions, the participants were increasing the amount of time spent together, but the results suggest that an intimate physical activity like cuddling has a greater potential to influence relationship health than a less intimate activity like eating together.

The takeaway

It's likely that both you and your spouse enjoy cuddling together, but it's often an activity that easily falls by the wayside if you're busy or tired. The results of this research suggest, however, that when you skimp on cuddling, you're depriving yourselves of not just an enjoyable activity but also a valuable tool that helps maintain and improve the quality of your relationship. One way to make sure that it doesn't get deprioritized is to incorporate it into your daily schedule. You might, for instance, agree to head to bed twenty minutes before you normally do, put away the screens and the books, turn off the TV, and give yourselves the opportunity to be physically close with each other, even if it doesn't lead to more amorous activity. Although, who knows? It might!

A KISS BEFORE PARTING

Among married couples, a shared bed is by far the most common sleeping arrangement. In a 2013 poll about sleep habits, more than 80 percent of people with a significant other said they share a bed with their partner. Some couples do, however, opt to sleep in separate rooms, typically because they find it results in better-quality sleep for each of them. If you're considering such an arrangement, remember that spending quality time together before lights out can help you feel more like a married couple and less like mere housemates, so consider cuddling or exchanging a good-night kiss in one of the bedrooms before parting ways.

PART 7

USE YOUR SENSES

Research Areas:

LANGUAGE   PERCEPTION

🧪 The experiment

You'll need paper and pencils for this one. Each of you will be given four sentences, and you must draw a doodle that represents each sentence. Flip a coin to determine who will be Illustrator A and who will be Illustrator B. Illustrator A should turn to page 250 to read their instructions, and Illustrator B should turn to page 258 for their instructions.

❓ The hypothesis

Illustrator A is more likely to answer Friday than Monday. Illustrator B has about an equal chance of choosing Friday or Monday.

🔬 The research

Normally, when we talk about motion, we mean literal physical motion. But it's common to find examples of language where the motion described is only metaphorical. This type of usage, called fictive motion, applies to things that don't physically move, such as a fence that is said to "run" along the perimeter of a house.

In a 2005 study, researchers wanted to see whether exposing people to examples of fictive motion might influence how they think about time. Half of study participants were asked to draw the scenes described in List A, where fictive motion is used, and the other half were asked to draw the scenes described in List B, where fictive motion is not used. Then the participants were asked the question about the rescheduled meeting. About 70 percent of those in the fictive-motion group answered Friday. In the other group, participants were equally split between Monday and Friday.

The researchers think that when people are primed to think about this metaphorical type of motion, they're more likely to use the same way of thinking about time and "move" the date forward to Friday.

(!) The takeaway

It can be hard to talk about nonphysical concepts, so we often borrow phrases that apply to more concrete things and use them in a metaphorical sense. You may find that as a couple, talking about abstract concepts or emotionally charged subjects requires the same sort of effort. When you find yourself struggling to communicate, think about something that's concrete and familiar to your spouse—for instance, a car for an auto enthusiast or a garden for a nature lover—and look for opportunities to make helpful analogies. Not only does it show that you're attuned to their interests, but it may also be the key to getting your point across.

41

MUSIC STYLE STEREOTYPES

Research Areas:

MUSIC   PERSONALITY

 **The experiment**

You and your spouse should each separately answer the following prompts about different aspects of your personalities, using a scale from 1 (strongly disagree) to 10 (strongly agree):

I am satisfied with my existing number of friends. ____

Few of my friends are outgoing. ____

I consider myself to be religious. ____

I regularly recycle bottles, cans, paper, and old clothes. ____

My politics lean conservative. ____

Next, from the following list, choose the musical style you most enjoy.

A. Opera   **E.** Top 40   **I.** Hip-hop

B. Country   **F.** Musicals   **J.** Dance

C. Classical   **G.** Indie   **K.** Electronica

D. Blues   **H.** Rock   **L.** R&B

The hypothesis

If you selected a musical style from the first column, you are more likely to have given high-value answers to the five prompts. If you selected a musical style from the third column, you are most likely to have given low-value answers to the prompts. If you selected a musical style from the center column, your answers to the prompts probably fell in the middle of the range.

 The research

Researchers in a 2007 study sought to investigate whether musical preferences were associated with personality traits, behavior, or lifestyle attributes. They analyzed more than 2,000 responses to a questionnaire that asked participants about their musical preferences, interpersonal relationships, religious views, political views, and other personal beliefs and attributes.

They found that respondents could generally be lumped into three broad categories. The first, which included fans of opera, country, classical, and blues, tended to be more conservative and less defiant in various aspects of their life. The second, which included fans of hip-hop, dance, electronic, and R&B music, tended to be more liberal and more defiant. Fans of the remaining styles tended to be somewhere in the middle.

The study did not examine any causal relationships between these qualities and preferences, so the researchers refrained from making assertions about whether enjoying any particular type of music leads a person to behave in a certain way or like certain things; whether behavior and personal preferences influence musical preferences; or whether there are hidden variables at play that make a direct causal relationship unlikely.

(!) The takeaway

Although the study did identify a variety of associations between musical preferences and other personal qualities, it's worth noting that participants were only able to select one favorite music style from among multiple possibilities. So unless you're a walking stereotype, you probably enjoy musical genres that span across the columns. You might be a fan of both classical and hip-hop. Your spouse might like country and R&B (which, by the way, share similar roots). Or you might be one of the many people who defies the general association: an opera lover who's antiauthoritarian, or a heavy metal aficionado who's also a gentle homebody. Just remember that even if musical preferences might have some slight predictive value in the aggregate, your own personal tastes are unique, and the combined tastes between you and your spouse result in a one-of-a-kind match.

42

AUDIO ANALGESICS

Research Areas:

MUSIC   PAIN

🧪 The experiment

Each of you should select, and queue up on a music player, one or more of your favorite songs. Next, gather a stopwatch and a bucket full of ice water that is big enough that you can submerge your hand in it. Now it's time to test your pain tolerance. Using the stopwatch, time how long each of you can keep your nondominant hand submerged in the ice water. Once you've both completed the trial, take a break and do a short, distracting task together—such as folding laundry, tidying a bookshelf, or slow-dancing in your living room—and then return to

the bowl of ice water. Repeat the task, but this time you should listen to your chosen song as you hold your hand underwater.

Tweak it

If you're willing to perform the task a third time and don't mind using some salty language, flip a coin to determine which spouse should be the Swearer and which should be the Non-Swearer. The Swearer should select a curse word and repeat it while holding their hand in the ice water. The Non-Swearer should do the same, but repeat a neutral word, such as "duck!"

❓ The hypothesis

You will be able to keep your hand in the ice water longer the second time around, when you are listening to music, compared to your first attempt.

🔬 The research

You and your spouse have just performed a version of a "cold pressor" test, which involves dunking your hand in a bucket of ice water. The task is often used to measure people's pain tolerance. In a 2006 study, researchers examined whether distractions such as music, math, or stand-up comedy might help participants better tolerate the cold pressor task. Their results showed that listening to music during the task allowed the participants to keep their hands submerged longer than doing distracting math problems or listening to a stand-up comedy album, even though people in all three conditions rated the intensity of the pain roughly the same. A 2011 study backed up this conclusion and found that music that was positive in mood but low in energy, evoking contentment rather than exuberance, was most effective as a distractor during the cold pressor test.

Did you try the tweaked version of the experiment involving dirty and clean words? A 2009 study investigated whether swearing acts as a coping mechanism for pain. Researchers split participants into two groups. One group repeated a swear word during the cold pressor task, and the other group repeated a neutral word. The researchers found that swearing increased people's pain tolerance, allowing them to hold their hands underwater longer, and also decreased the perceived intensity of the pain they experienced. This held true for just about everyone, they noted, except for "males with a tendency to catastrophize."

(!) The takeaway

It's a safe bet that each of you will experience moments of pain during your marriage. For minor pain, a little Tylenol might do the trick, but sometimes there's just no way to wipe out the pain completely. In those cases, distraction strategies, such as listening to upbeat music, might not decrease the intensity of the pain, but they might make it a little easier to tolerate. Then there will be times when even distraction strategies can't cut it. The pain might be so raw and so intense that it's practically all you can think about. In such moments, it's important for your partner to remember that they may not be able to ease your pain, but they can be there for you, gripping your hand, wiping your brow, encouraging you not to despair, or simply sitting quietly beside you. Pain is not always within our control, but devotion certainly is.

43
BLIND CHOICE

Research Areas:

DECISION MAKING   PREFERENCES

🧪 The experiment

If you weren't able to visit a far-flung destination on your honeymoon, now's your chance to dream about it. Flip a coin to determine who will act as the Travel Agent and who will be the Vacation Chooser. Once you've figured out who will fill each role, the Vacation Chooser should briefly leave the room, and the Travel Agent should read on.

You will need to gather two blank index cards. On each card, write in illegible handwriting a nonsense word that's between six and ten letters long. Place the index cards down on a table so the writing is facing down. You should also come up with two countries that your spouse would have an equivalent desire to visit.

When you call your spouse back into the room, you will have to engage in some mild deception. Don't worry—at the end of the project you can come clean and explain the true nature of the experiment.

Tell your partner that you are going to do a simple exercise to test a theory about subliminal decision-making. Say that you are going to very briefly display two index cards simultaneously, one in your left hand and one in your right, each with the name of a vacation destination on it. Explain that the cards will be shown so briefly that your spouse will be unable to consciously grasp the names of the destinations. Nevertheless, they should trust their subconscious mind and indicate, by pointing to a card, which vacation destination they would prefer to visit.

Now, briefly lift up the index cards with a quick up-and-down motion in such a way that your partner cannot possibly read the words written on each card. Then prompt them to choose a card.

Remember the two country names you brainstormed earlier? Tell your spouse that those two countries were the two options written on the cards, and the second country was the one they selected. Then prompt your spouse to rate, on a scale from 1 to 10, how interested they are in visiting each of the two destinations.

😲 The hypothesis

Your spouse will give a higher rating to the second destination, the one they were told that their subconscious mind preferred.

🔬 The research

Psychologists have observed for quite some time that the mere act of making a choice appears to alter our preferences. Starting with a seminal 1956 study and replicated in multiple subsequent studies, researchers have shown that participants who initially rate two options as being roughly equal in value will, after choosing one over the other, rate the chosen option higher than they originally did, and rate the other option lower.

In 2009, a pair of social psychology researchers argued that all of these free-choice experiments assume the initial rating reflects the person's true preference and the post-choice rating reflects an altered preference. But it may be the case that the post-choice rating better reflects the person's true preference, and the initial rating was less accurate because it had not been fine-tuned through the process of deliberation.

The authors of a 2010 study set out to disprove this idea. They designed an experiment in which participants made a choice, but it was essentially a blind choice, because they were not aware of the two options they were choosing from and thus could not deliberate between them.

At the beginning of the experiment, participants rated a number of travel destinations. Then, as in the experiment you just performed with your spouse, their experiment briefly showed the participants nonsense characters that were purportedly the names of two vacation destinations. The participants then had to choose one of the two possibilities. Then the researchers revealed the names of two destinations that the participants had previously rated similarly and told the participants that one of the two destinations was the option they had selected. The participants then rated the two possibilities, and the "chosen" destination was rated higher on average than the "rejected" destination.

The 2010 study's authors argue that these results give weight to the idea that it really is the act of choosing that alters our preferences, because if post-choice ratings were a better measure of a person's true preferences than pre-choice ratings, as the 2009 researchers had suggested, then this "blind choice" experiment, in which the choice is essentially a random one, would not have led to an increase in post-choice ratings, because there was no way for those true preferences to affect the decision-making.

Why do we value a chosen option higher after choosing it? One possible explanation the researchers offer is that it helps us commit to our choices, rather than wasting time second-guessing ourselves or dwelling on what might have been.

(!) The takeaway

You and your spouse will likely face some decisions where you're genuinely torn between the possibilities and can't seem to agree on which is the best. It might be a relatively inconsequential decision, like where to spend a weekend away, or a relatively life-changing choice, like whether to move across the country or across the world for a new job. In such cases, it might actually help both of you make a decision by doing what you did at the start of this project: flipping a coin.

Once you've made the decision and committed to it, you will have freed yourselves from the limbo of back-and-forth deliberations, allowing you to move on and make further plans. If the results of this research are any indication, you will feel glad for having done so, no matter which side the coin landed on.

MUNCH MANIPULATION

The experiment

This project calls for a female research subject, so bride, read no further. Your spouse is in charge of setting up this project.

You will conduct the experiment over two evenings; they don't need to be consecutive. On each night, gather a low-calorie snack, such as grapes, and a high-calorie snack, such as potato chips, and place them in similar-sized bowls. On the first night, select a half-hour TV show that your wife is likely to find watchable, but somewhat boring, such as a documentary or lecture. Place both bowls in an accessible place and allow her to snack freely from both bowls. Keep an eye on how much of each

 type of snack she eats. On the second night, you'll make the same two snacks available, but this time, choose a half-hour comedy that your spouse is likely to find funny and highly engaging. Again, keep an eye on how much of each type of snack she eats.

⑦ The hypothesis

Your wife is likely to eat more overall during the boring viewing session than during the engaging viewing session. The amount of potato chips she consumes during each of the two sessions will be roughly the same, but she'll eat more grapes during the boring session.

⑧ The research

Television watching tends to be an activity during which people eat out of habit, not necessarily out of hunger. A 2014 study sought to determine whether the degree to which the viewer is bored or engaged with the content affects consumption. The study's authors decided to recruit only women as participants, since previous research had shown that women tend to be more restrained in their eating habits than men, so it is easier to experimentally manipulate their restraint level.

The women watched either a boring art lecture or an engaging comedy for thirty minutes and were permitted to snack on bowls of M&Ms and grapes. The researchers found that although the women in each condition ate roughly the same amount of M&Ms, those in the boring condition ate about 60 percent more grapes than those in the engaging condition.

The results of the study demonstrate that it may not be TV watching itself that leads people to go overboard with snacking. Rather, it might be the emotional state the viewing content induces that prompts people to eat more.

(!) The takeaway

There will probably be times when the two of you want nothing more than to veg on the couch together and watch some mindless TV. The results of this study suggest that watching highly engaging shows or movies is not only entertaining but also good for your waistline. Then again, the difference in eating between the boring and engaging condition consisted mostly of a healthy food, so it may be the case that although boring content leads people to eat more than engaging content, they're eating more of a healthy food—which might have benefits that outweigh the extra calories consumed. Of course, if you're really concerned about your diet, the best thing to do is skip the dual options and serve yourself only healthy snacks. Better yet, turn off the TV and find a less sedentary activity to pass the time.

GENDERED MEAL PREFERENCES

The preceding project was adapted from a study that recruited only female participants, because earlier research had shown that women tend to be more susceptible to experimental manipulation of their eating habits.

That's not the only gender difference when it comes to diet.

A 2015 study looked at whether people are more or less likely to choose a stereotypically masculine menu item (a hamburger) over a stereotypically feminine menu item (a Caprese salad) when they are dining with someone of their own sex versus someone of the opposite sex. Male participants adapted their choice to the sex of their dining partner. When dining with a man, they were more likely to choose the burger, and when dining with a woman, they were more likely to choose the salad. Women, on the other hand, preferred the salad regardless of their dining partner's gender, although they did report that they would be more willing to eat a burger if their dining partner were a man than a woman.

The study's authors say the results support the idea that women feel more social pressure to conform to gender stereotypes about food choices than men do.

PART 8

COMPARE OPINIONS

45

HUMOR ME

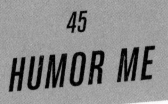

Research Areas: HUMOR   RELATIONSHIP QUALITY

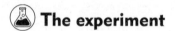 The experiment

Separately jot down your answers to the following eight statements. For each statement, answer on a scale from 1 (not at all) to 10 (very much):

1. My spouse uses humor to amuse other people, e.g., joke telling and witty banter. ____

2. My spouse uses humor to improve his/her own mood, e.g., thinking about funny situations. ____

3. My spouse uses humor to criticize, e.g., sarcasm, teasing, or ridicule. ____

4. My spouse uses humor to produce laughter at his/her own expense, e.g., self-deprecating jokes. ____

5. I expect more good things to happen to me than
bad. ____

6. I strongly believe that I will achieve the goals I've set
for myself. ____

7. I have a cheerful effect on others. ____

8. I feel that I am not especially in control of my life.

____

The hypothesis

Your answers to the first four statements about your spouse's humor style will predict your answers to the last four statements about optimism and happiness. Specifically, higher-value statements to questions 1 and 2, and lower-value statements to questions 3 and 4, are associated with higher overall happiness and optimism, which is measured by high-value answers to statements 5–7 and a low-value answer to statement 8.

The research

Three researchers conducted a 2011 study that examined the ways in which perceived and self-reported humor styles were associated with relationship satisfaction among young, committed couples. They classified humor styles into four groups: humor primarily intended to positively affect the mood of others; humor primarily intended to positively affect one's own mood; humor primarily intended to belittle others; and humor primarily intended to belittle oneself. (These four humor style correspond to the first four statements you answered at the beginning of this experiment.)

During the study, the researchers asked couples to describe both their own humor style and their partner's humor style, and then to complete a relationship assessment. Humor styles were categorized based on the four groups, and then the researchers looked to see whether particular styles were associated with relationship satisfaction.

They found that many couples had differing humor styles, and a difference did not seem to indicate incompatibility. However, relationship satisfaction was most strongly associated with the two humor styles that are directed at others (either to amuse or belittle). The more a participant perceived their partner as using humor to amuse others, the stronger the reported satisfaction, and the more they perceived their partner as using humor to belittle others, the lesser the reported satisfaction. The study found a milder effect with the two self-focused humor styles, where humor used to amuse oneself was associated with higher satisfaction and humor used to belittle oneself was associated with lower satisfaction.

Do these humor styles only affect relationship satisfaction? No, they seem to have wide-ranging associations. For instance, a 2008 study found that the two positive humor styles are also associated with measures of general happiness and optimism.

(ⓘ) The takeaway

Regardless of your humor styles, it's important to realize that you don't need to have the same style as your spouse to be compatible. But if either of you leans heavily on aggressive humor that puts down others to build yourself up, watch out! Not only can it earn you plenty of enemies, but it might also drag down your relationship. Insult comedy may have its place on the stage, but when you're spending time with your spouse, the only roasting you should be doing is preparing the main course for a romantic meal.

COMIC, OR SANS?

Both men and women tend to rank a sense of humor high on their list of desirable qualities in a mate, but it turns out they have different preferences for how that sense of humor is expressed. A 2006 study found that women placed equal value on men who are receptive to their own humor and men who are skilled at cracking jokes themselves. Men, on the other hand, preferred women who are receptive to their own humor, but they were essentially indifferent about whether the woman is funny herself.

46
SUCH A TEASE

Research Areas:

HUMOR   PERSONALITY   RELATIONSHIP QUALITY

 **The experiment**

Each of you should think of two episodes when teasing occurred in your relationship. For one of those episodes, choose a time when you teased your partner, and for the other, choose a time when your partner teased you. Altogether, you'll have recalled four separate episodes. It doesn't matter how long ago the episodes occurred, but both of you should be able to recall the basic details of each episode.

Now, separately, each of you should answer the following questions, using a scale from 1 (very low) to 10 (very high), for all four episodes:

How humorous was this tease? ____

How lighthearted was it? ____

To what extent was it given with good intentions? _____

How obvious do you think it was to the recipient that

    the teaser was just kidding? _____

How important do you think it was to the recipient that

    the teaser was just kidding? _____

❓ The hypothesis

Regardless of who chose the teasing episode, the spouse who was the teaser is likely to have given higher ratings for all five questions than the spouse who was the recipient of the tease.

The research

Lighthearted teasing—the kind that's not intended to hurt the recipient's feelings—is an art that, if poorly practiced, can be misinterpreted and cause lasting damage to relationships. That's because this form of teasing is inherently sarcastic, and if the recipient doesn't pick up on the sarcasm, you're in for it.

    The tease itself, which can range from a subtle ribbing to a dripping dagger, is always negative. But the broader context, including how you say it and the strength of your relationship with the recipient, should convey that the words aren't meant to offend, but instead spring from a sense of affection. However, it's easy for teasers to misjudge the extent to which the recipient appreciates the joke.

Researchers in a 2006 study sought to identify just how wide a rift exists between teasers, who see their teases as playful jabs, and recipients, who might not appreciate the jabs, playful or not. They studied teasing behavior among several groups, including roommates, friends and family, and romantic couples. Pairs from each group were asked to recall instances in which they had teased or been teased by the other person, and to rate the episodes with a variation of the questions you answered earlier. Among all the groups studied, the researchers found that teasers considered their teases to be more humorous, more lighthearted, more good-natured, and more obviously a joke than did the recipients. This, the authors suggest, is indicative of the fact that it is a difficult task for the subject of a tease to know quite how the teaser intended it. But in a related experiment in which the teaser's good intentions were made clearer, the teasers were still more likely than the teased to say that intent matters. In other words, if you're the one being teased, you're less likely than the teaser might expect to forgive the tease simply because it was intended as a joke.

(!) The takeaway

Teasing comes naturally to many couples. You might, for instance, tease your beloved about minor idiosyncrasies, thinking that the trivial insult is unlikely to cause damage and that your spouse knows you don't mean to be hurtful. But tread very carefully, because good intentions can't fully make up for a poorly conceived potshot. If you just can't break yourself of the teasing habit, or you're skeptical of its potential for harm, then at least limit the chance for misunderstanding by making very clear that your tease is all in good fun. Don't be surprised, though, if occasionally you get a stiff jab in return.

47

SODA STICKER SHOCK

```
┌─────────────────────────────────────────────┐
│         Research Area:  ⚖                     │
│                        MORALITY               │
└─────────────────────────────────────────────┘
```

🧪 The experiment

Flip a coin to decide who will read Scenario A and who will read Scenario B. The spouse assigned to Scenario A should turn to page 251 to read the scenario. The spouse assigned to Scenario B should turn to page 258 to read the scenario.

Once you have both finished reading your scenarios, you should individually answer the following questions, using a scale of 1 (not at all) to 10 (extremely):

How fair do you consider this vending machine? ____
To what degree would this vending machine make you
    feel cheated? ____
To what degree would this vending machine make you
    feel angry? ____

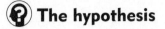 The hypothesis

The spouse who read Scenario B, which described the vending machine trial as occurring one month in the future, will consider it to be more unfair, and will feel more cheated and angry about it, than the spouse who read Scenario A, which described the trial as having occurred one month in the past.

The research

It would seem as if whether an unfair action happens in the past or the future should have no bearing on its degree of unfairness. But a 2010 study found that in multiple experiments, participants judged future unfairness more harshly than unfairness that occurred in the past. In one such experiment, participants were split into two groups. Both read about a vending machine trial in which the machine increased its prices as the weather got hotter, but one group was told that the trial had already occurred, whereas the other group was told it would occur soon. Those in the future condition found the trial to be less fair, and reported that it made them feel more negative emotions, than those in the past condition.

The study's author suggests that people have a stronger reaction to the future condition because they know that at least some future events can be averted through action (such as through a letter-writing campaign or by boycotting a business), whereas no past events can be undone. Thus, even in the case where we know we can't influence a future event, we may nevertheless feel a heightened moral and emotional response to it, simply because the future, in general, is less certain than the past. This has a variety of practical and moral implications. For instance, viewing past events less severely might help facilitate forgiveness. And if future events are seen through a harsher moral lens, then there might be some truth to the adage attributed to famed computer scientist Grace Hopper: "It is easier to ask forgiveness than permission."

(!) The takeaway

The ability to impose moral and emotional leniency on past actions may help you resolve incidents of bad behavior, but remember that there are some potential downsides to the lopsided way we view past and future events. If we know that it's easier to ask for forgiveness from our spouse than to ask permission, how does that affect our conduct? Does it make us more likely to take advantage of the situation and engage in behavior we know our spouse would not like? Hopefully not! Particularly now that you've both had a chance to learn about this research, it's worth having a frank discussion about why that sort of subversive behavior is itself damaging to the relationship, over and above the bad conduct itself.

48

EXCUSES, EXCUSES

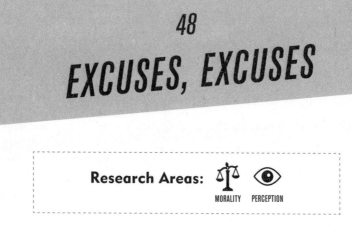

Research Areas: MORALITY   PERCEPTION

 **The experiment**

Flip a coin to decide which spouse will read about the Baker and which spouse will read about the Driver.

The spouse who will read about the Baker should turn to page 251. The spouse who will read about the Driver should turn to page 259.

The hypothesis

The spouse who read the scenario about Erin, the baker, is just as likely to have answered "Yes" as they are to have answered "No" to the second question. And the spouse who read the scenario about Luke, the driver, is highly likely to have circled "Luke unintentionally broke the rules," but pretty unlikely to have circled "Luke broke the rules," when given the opportunity to select multiple true statements. However, when that spouse turned to the follow-up question, which demanded a yes-or-no answer, they are likely to have answered "Yes" to "Did Luke break the rules?"

The research

A study published in 2014 examined what might lead people to excuse rule breaking. In one experiment, participants read a scenario similar to the one about the baker. All of the participants acknowledged that the rules of the baking contest prohibited artificial sweeteners, and that the baker had unknowingly used artificial sweetener, yet only about half of them were willing to agree that there was some sense in which the baker had done something incorrect.

The researchers suggested that the participants were excusing the rule breaking because saying that the baker had done something incorrect might be perceived as an indirect way of criticizing the baker, and people are reluctant to criticize a person for something that's not actually their fault.

So, in another experiment, a similar scenario was presented, but the researchers tweaked the questions that participants were asked. The participants were presented with three statements, in which the protagonist was described as having broken the rules; having unintentionally broken the rules; and having not broken the rules. They were permitted to select one or more of the statements that applied to the scenario. Then, they were ushered into a different room, so they could not change their previous answers, and asked directly: Did the person break the rules?

The researchers found that when the multiple choices were presented, the vast majority of people agreed that the person had unintentionally broken the rules, but less than a quarter of them also said that the person had broken the rules, even though they had been prompted to select all options that applied. Yet when the participants later answered the direct yes-or-no question, 83 percent agreed that the person had broken the rules.

The researchers think that because the participants in this second experiment were given the option during the first round of questions to indicate that the rule breaking was unintentional, they were freed from the dilemma faced by the people who'd read the baker scenario: Do you say that the person broke the rules, which might unfairly imply that they are to blame, or do you say that they didn't break the rules, which does not unfairly blame but isn't technically true? In the baker scenario, about half of the people resolved that dilemma by fudging the truth, rather than implying criticism. But in the second experiment, since the participants were able to indicate that the rule breaking was unintentional during the first round of questions, they later felt more comfortable acknowledging that the rules had, indeed, been broken, because they'd already had a chance to clarify that they knew the rule breaking was not the protagonist's fault.

(!) The takeaway

The early-twentieth-century author G. K. Chesterton once wrote: "Men do not differ much about what things they will call evils; they differ enormously about what evils they will call excusable." Although the scenarios you considered were cases where the protagonist was clearly not at fault for breaking a rule, there are other, more murky situations where it's not quite as evident. It can be tempting, in some such scenarios, to rationalize or excuse the rule breaking—especially if it's you who is breaking the rules. For married couples, there's an additional temptation to excuse a spouse's rule breaking. The results of this study suggest that when we are able to separate our judgment about a person's culpability from our judgment about whether the person has done something incorrect, it can be easier to acknowledge the latter. Perhaps your well-meaning spouse has washed an item of your clothing that you knew to be dry-clean only, but which is not clearly labeled as such, and ruined it in the process. You might want to begin the conversation by pointing out that you know your spouse was only trying to help, and it's understandable that they failed to realize the item needed to be professionally cleaned. Once you've started the conversation on the right note, it can be easier for both of you to acknowledge the reality of the situation and work toward a satisfying resolution.

49

PARENTAL PEEVES

Research Area:
FAMILIAL
RELATIONSHIPS

🧪 The experiment

Each of you should individually complete the following questions about your relationship with your parent or parents, and specifically about tension in that relationship. For the purposes of these questions, tension means that either you or your parent is bothered by an issue, even if you've never directly argued about it. For each question, respond using a scale from 0 (not at all) to 10 (a great deal):

1. **In the past year, my relationship with my parent(s) has experienced tension regarding:**

    My housekeeping ____

    My career or education ____

My financial decisions ____

My healthcare decisions ____

My lifestyle decisions ____

Their housekeeping ____

Their career or education ____

Their financial decisions ____

Their healthcare decisions ____

Their lifestyle decisions ____

2. **In the past year, my relationship with my parent(s) has experienced tension regarding:**

   Frequency of contact/communication ____

   Personality differences ____

   Unsolicited advice ____

   Past relationship problems ____

3. **Regarding my relationship with my parent(s):**

   I trust them. ____

   I understand them. ____

   I respect them. ____

   I feel affection toward them. ____

   I consider them to be fair. ____

4. **Regarding my relationship with my parent(s):**

They make me feel loved. ____

They understand me. ____

They criticize me. ____

They make demands on me. ____

Once you've chosen values for the four statements in question set 4, you'll need to compute your Ambivalence Score, which will be a value between 0 and 10. Combine the values from the first two statements in set 4 to get your Positive Score. Combine the values from the other two statements in set 4 to get your Negative Score. Subtract the smaller score from the larger score, add 1, and multiply by 2 to get your Difference Value. Then add both the Positive and Negative Scores together to get your Sum Value. Finally, divide the Sum by the Difference to get your Ambivalence Score.

⑦ The hypothesis

Your answers in question set 1 pertain to tension caused by the individual behavior of you and your parent(s), and your answers in question set 2 pertain to tension caused by the parent-child relationship itself. Low values in these first two question sets predict high values in question set 3, which measures positive sentiments toward your parents, and a low Ambivalence Score. High values in the first two question sets predict low values in question set 3 and a high Ambivalence Score. Between question set 1 and question set 2, the latter will have the strongest link to the overall quality of the relationship.

The research

In a 2009 study involving parents and their adult children, both the parents and the children rated the level of tension in their parent-child relationship on a number of issues, which were broadly divided into two categories: those related to the behavior of either a parent or an adult child, and those related to the parent-child relationship itself. Participants also answered questions to measure the positive sentiments they felt toward their parent or child, as well as their level of ambivalence, or conflicted positive and negative feelings, about their familial relationship.

The study's authors found that tensions related to the parent-child relationship itself were more closely tied to relationship quality than tensions related to the behavior of one of the family members. The presence of individual tensions did, however, lead to more feelings of ambivalence. Why would relationship tensions be more detrimental than individual tensions to the quality of the parent-child relationship? The researchers suggest that it may be because the frustration with individual tensions, such as lifestyle or career choices, is frequently left unspoken, whereas it is harder to hide one's feelings about issues like personality differences or unsolicited advice.

A related 2009 study by some of the same authors explored how parents and their adult children coped with relationship tension. They found, perhaps unsurprisingly, that destructive strategies, such as put-downs, and avoidance strategies, like not talking about an irritating behavior, were associated with poorer relationship quality, but constructive strategies, which attempt to directly resolve conflicts in a positive way, were associated with enhanced relationship quality.

(!) The takeaway

It's common to talk of parents of a bride or groom "giving away" their adult child at the altar, but for many families, a wedding can be an impetus for making the parental bond stronger. That doesn't mean, however, that you and your spouse will always see eye to eye with your parents or in-laws. The results of this research show that the tensions that are most likely to damage your family bonds are those related to the relationship itself, so if preserving or rekindling a good relationship with parents or in-laws is important to you, put the effort into sustaining it just as you would any close relationship. If they live nearby, make sure they see you often. If they don't, make sure they get regular phone calls, texts, or emails. Acknowledge and try to appreciate personality differences, and avoid digging up past conflicts. That can sometimes be a tall order, so lean on your spouse for support and encouragement during the tense times, and be sure to celebrate successes together.

POLL YOUR PARENTS

Feeling especially daring? Ask your parents to complete the same questionnaire you completed about them, but with their answers about *you*. Then, compare their answers to yours. What should you expect to see? In the original study, the researchers found that parents and adult children were roughly on the same page about relationship tensions (those from question set 2), but parents tended to report greater individual tensions (those from question set 1) than their adult children did. The researchers point out that this is consistent with research on the relationship between parents and adolescent children: tensions are more likely to bother parents than teenagers, and teens recover more quickly from parent-child conflicts. It appears that these differing perceptions of and reactions to tension extend past adolescence and continue after the child reaches adulthood. If a strong relationship with your parents or in-laws is important to you and an achievable goal, then bearing in mind how keenly parents feel these tensions can help you approach both direct conflicts and unspoken stress or strain with sensitivity and grace.

50
THERMO-COUPLING

Research Area:
CONSUMER
PSYCHOLOGY

🧪 The experiment

Together, come up with a list of twelve movies that the two of you are familiar with. They can be movies you have already seen or wish to see. Include three comedies, three action movies, three romances, and three thrillers. Write the titles of all twelve films on two separate sheets of paper.

Now, flip a coin to determine who should be in the Warm condition and who should be in the Cool condition.

The spouse who is in the Warm condition should take one of the sheets of paper and complete the next part of the project in a relatively warm environment. If you're reading this during the summer, go outside in the sun. If it's winter, go indoors, sit by a heat vent, and drink a hot beverage.

Meanwhile, the spouse who is in the Cool condition should take the other sheet of paper and complete the next part of the project in a relatively cool environ-ment. If you're reading this during the summer, turn your air conditioner on full blast and drink an iced tea. If it's winter, go outside.

Once you're in your designated environment, go through the list of twelve movie titles and rate each one based on your level of interest in that movie right now, using a scale from 1 (very low) to 10 (very high).

The hypothesis

The spouse in the Cool condition will be more likely to want to watch the romance films than the spouse in the Warm condition.

The research

Cunning teenage Romeos have discovered that surreptitiously lowering the thermostat a few degrees when watching a movie with a date encourages closer snuggling. It turns out that feeling a chill in the air not only encourages coziness on the couch, but it also influences our genre preferences.

A 2011 study asked participants to indicate their level of interest in a variety of movies from different genres. Some participants completed their questionnaires in a warm room or were prompted to drink a hot beverage while answering the questions; others completed their questionnaires in a cool room or were prompted to drink a cold beverage.

The results showed that physical coldness led to increased interest in romance movies. This increase did not apply to the other three categories: action, comedy, or thriller. As part of the same study, the authors analyzed an online movie rental data set along with historical weather data to see whether decreases in outside temperatures led to increases in rentals of romance films. Their analysis confirmed their suspicions: cold weather predicted customers' interest in romance films, but not films in other genres.

Why would our interest in romance films increase as temperatures drop? The study's authors suggest that a feeling of physical coldness leads us to desire psychological warmth, and watching romance films, with their emotional plotlines and mostly happy endings, is like a mug of hot cocoa for the soul.

(!) The takeaway

Hollywood has taken notice of consumers' preferences, which is why many romantic comedies and dramas are released between November and February. It helps that Christmas (which itself arouses sentimental feelings) and Valentine's Day both occur during the winter season. If you're the type who likes romantic films any time of the year, but your spouse has more seasonally influenced viewing preferences, one way you can get your fix of sappy flicks is to turn down the heat as the two of you make a decision about what to watch. If the movie is steamy enough, it might lead you both to turn up the heat without having to adjust the thermostat.

5. TIME WEALTHINESS

Self-Focused Task: Please take fifteen to twenty minutes today to do something for yourself that you weren't already planning to do.

10. A REMOTE CHANCE

Spouse A Instructions: You have been asked to participate in a promotional campaign for a national bookstore chain. Two prize packages will be described. If you opt into the promotion for a prize package, you have a very high chance of winning that prize. For each of the two prizes, write down, on a scale from 1 (not at all interested) to 10 (extremely interested), your interest level in participating in the promotion.

12. THE MIND'S EYE

A

B

C

D

E

F

14. TRIP THE SCRIPT

Answer Key: True, False, False, False, True, False, True, False, False, True

15. ON A POSITIVE NOTE

Special Instructions for Interviewer: While your spouse recounts the details of the Focus Event, your goal is to be an active, constructive listener. During the course of the story your spouse tells, you should express enthusiastic, positive verbal feedback, such as "That's great," or "I'm really happy that happened to you." You should also give positive nonverbal cues, such as smiling, nodding, and making eye contact with your spouse.

17. MENTAL PICTURES

SHOE

PENCIL

EAGLE

EGG

MITT

BOOK

18. MISS QUOTA

Contestant A Instructions: In this game, you and your spouse will be given five sets of jumbled letters. You will have five minutes to write down as many dictionary words as possible that can be formed from any of the five sets of jumbled letters. You will earn one point for each dictionary word you identify. Once time is up, add up all of your points and announce your score to your spouse.

19. CHUGGING CHALLENGE

Chugger A Instructions: If you are able to drink all of the water in your container within two minutes, you will win the larger reward.

20. DISTORTED TRUTHS
First Round:

1. How many of each animal did Moses take on the ark?
2. Which country is famous for cuckoo clocks, banks, and pocketknives?
3. Who does Clark Kent become when he changes in a tollbooth?
4. What phrase followed "To be or not to be" in Macbeth's famous soliloquy?
5. What English rock group did the late John Lennon sing with?

23. KARAOKE CHALLENGE

Singer A Instructions: People think that feeling anxious about singing in public will make them sing poorly. However, recent research suggests that anxiety doesn't hurt singing performance and can even help performance. People who feel anxious about singing might actually do better. This means that you shouldn't feel concerned if you do feel anxious while performing your song. If you find yourself feeling anxious, simply remind yourself that your anxiety could be helping you do well. As you step up to the microphone, think to yourself, "I am excited about singing!"

28. GOOD, BAD, AND BETTER THAN OTHERS

Instructions A: The following questions examine how your relationship may be similar to or different than other people's relationships. As you answer them, please be as honest and as accurate as you possibly can:

1. What features of romantic relationships and partners do you think of as good and desirable? If you think a particular feature is more typical of your relationship or partner than of other people's, place a check mark next to that feature.

2. What features of romantic relationships and partners do you think of as bad and undesirable? If you think a particular feature is more typical of your relationship or partner than of other people's, place a check mark next to that feature.

29. HIGHS AND LOWS

"Why" Condition Instructions: Write a brief, one-sentence response to the following statement: "Why do I maintain good physical health?" The response should take the form, "Because I _____." Then, take your answer and turn it into another

"Why" question: "Why do I _____?" Answer it with a second "Because I _____" statement. Do this two more times, so you have four answers total.

31. JOTTING THANKS

Extra Assignment: During the weekly period between each questionnaire, you should write a letter of gratitude to a specific person in your life, letting them know how much they mean to you. The letters should not be thank-you notes for material gifts, but rather letters that express your feelings of gratitude for your relationship with this person. Each of the three letters you write should be addressed to a different person. Please hold off on mailing the letters until the experiment is over.

32. MALLEABLE ME

Instructions A: Reflect back on the incident you described and write a few sentences, addressed to yourself, expressing compassion and understanding about the incident.

35. WHAT MIGHT HAVE BEEN

Factual Writing Prompt: How did you and your close friend meet? Describe the sequence of events that led to you meeting and becoming friends. What other details led to things turning out the way they did?

40. A MATTER OF TIME

Illustrator A Instructions: For each of the following four sentences, draw a doodle that represents the image:

The bike path runs along the creek.

The highway runs along the coast.

The county line runs along the river.

The tattoo runs along his spine.

Once you've drawn the doodles, write down your answer to the following question:

Next Wednesday's meeting has been moved forward two days. What day is the meeting now that it has been rescheduled?

47. SODA STICKER SHOCK

Scenario A: Last month, a major beverage company performed a trial of a soft drink vending machine that changes its price according to the temperature. On colder days, a can of soda cost only $1, but on the hottest days, the price rose above $3.

48. EXCUSES, EXCUSES

The Baker: Erin has entered a baking contest. The rules of the contest state that artificial sweeteners are not permitted as ingredients. Erin purchased a box of sugar, not knowing that the factory had made a mistake and put artificial sweetener in the box instead of sugar. Because she thought it was sugar, Erin used the ingredient in her recipe.

1. Should Erin be blamed for using artificial sweetener? (Y/N)
2. Is there a sense in which it is incorrect for Erin to use that sweetener? (Y/N)

5. TIME WEALTHINESS

Other-Focused Task: Please take fifteen to twenty minutes today to do something for someone else that you weren't already planning to do.

10. A REMOTE CHANCE

Spouse B Instructions: You have been asked to participate in a promotional campaign for a national bookstore chain. Two prize packages will be described. If you opt into the promotion for a prize package, you will have a 1 in 100 chance of winning that prize. For each of the two prizes, write down, on a scale from 1 (not at all interested) to 10 (extremely interested), your interest level in participating in the promotion.

12. THE MIND'S EYE

1

2

3

18. MISS QUOTA

Contestant B Instructions: In this game, you and your spouse will be given five sets of jumbled words. You will have five minutes to write down as many dictionary words as possible that can be formed from any of the jumbled words. For each of the five jumbled words, if you manage to form eight or more dictionary words from that jumbled word, you will earn eight points. Once time is up, add up all of your points and announce your score to your spouse.

19. CHUGGING CHALLENGE

Chugger B Instructions: If you are able to drink all of the water in your container within two minutes, you will then flip a coin to determine your reward. If it lands on heads, you'll earn the small reward. If it lands on tails, you'll earn the larger reward.

20. DISTORTED TRUTHS

Second Round:

1. Who does Clark Kent become when he changes in a tollbooth?

2. What English rock group did the late John Lennon sing with?

3. How many of each animal did Moses take on the ark?

4. What phrase followed "To be or not to be" in Macbeth's famous soliloquy?

5. Which country is famous for cuckoo clocks, banks, and pocketknives?

23. KARAOKE CHALLENGE

Singer B Instructions: It is normal for people to feel anxious about singing in public, as you are about to do. The goal of this experiment is to determine how a stressful situation, such as singing in public, affects your singing performance.

28. GOOD, BAD, AND BETTER THAN OTHERS

Instructions B: Research has shown that most newlyweds believe their marital satisfaction will remain stable or improve over the coming years, but on average, marital satisfaction declines over the first four years. The following questions examine how your relationship may be similar to or different than other people's relationships.

1. What features of romantic relationships and partners do you think of as good and desirable? If you think a particular feature is more typical of your relationship or partner than of other people's, place a check mark next to that feature.

2. What features of romantic relationships and partners do you think of as bad and undesirable? If you think a particular feature is more typical of your relationship or partner than of other people's, place a check mark next to that feature.

29. HIGHS AND LOWS

"How" Condition Instructions: Write a brief, one-sentence response to the following statement: "How do I maintain good physical health?" The response should take the form, "I _____." Then, take your answer and turn it into another "How" question: "How do I _____?" Answer it with a second "I _____" statement. Do this two more times, so you have four answers total.

32. MALLEABLE ME

Instructions B: Reflect back on the incident you described and write a few sentences, addressed to yourself, pointing out some of your positive qualities and accomplishments.

35. WHAT MIGHT HAVE BEEN

Counterfactual Writing Prompt: How did you and your close friend meet? Describe the sequence of events that led to you meeting and becoming friends. Then, describe all the ways that your paths might not have crossed, and how your life might have ended up differently if the two of you hadn't met at the time you did.

40. A MATTER OF TIME

Illustrator B Instructions: For each of the following four sentences, draw a doodle that represents the image:

> The bike path is next to the creek.
>
> The highway is next to the coast.
>
> The county line is next to the river.
>
> The tattoo is next to his spine.

Once you've drawn the doodles, write down your answer to the following question: Next Wednesday's meeting has been moved forward two days. What day is the meeting now that it has been rescheduled?

47. SODA STICKER SHOCK

Scenario B: One month from now, a major beverage company will perform a limited-time trial of a soft drink vending machine that changes its price according to the temperature. On colder days, a can of soda will cost only $1, but on the hottest days, the price will rise above $3.

48. EXCUSES, EXCUSES

The Driver: Luke is driving home from the auto shop, where he just had his car repaired. He does not want to break any traffic laws, so he obeys the speed limit of 55 mph. He doesn't know that the mechanic tampered with the speedometer, so it does not correctly measure the speed. As a result, Luke is actually traveling at 60 mph.

1. Which of the following statements describes Luke? Circle all that apply.

Luke broke the rules.
Luke unintentionally broke the rules.
Luke did not break the rules.

Once you have circled all the applicable statements in the question above, answer the yes or no question below.

2. Did Luke break the rules? (Y/N)

APPENDIX: PROJECTS BY RESEARCH AREA

Projects are listed by number and title.

REFERENCES

1. BONDING OVER BONDAGE

Aron, Arthur, Christina C. Norman, Elaine N. Aron, Colin McKenna, and Richard E. Heyman. "Couples' Shared Participation in Novel and Arousing Activities and Experienced Relationship Quality." *Journal of Personality and Social Psychology* 78.2 (2000): 273–84.

2. WISHFUL SEEING

Balcetis, Emily, and David Dunning. "Wishful Seeing: More Desired Objects Are Seen as Closer." *Psychological Science* 21.1 (2010): 147–52.

Durgin F. H., D. DeWald, S. Lechich, Z. Li, and Z. Ontiveros. "Action and Motivation: Measuring Perception or Strategies?" *Psychonomic Bulletin & Review* 18.6 (2011): 1077–82.

3. THE FLOATING ARM TRICK

Ghosh, Arko, John Rothwell, and Patrick Haggard. "Using Voluntary Motor Commands to Inhibit Involuntary Arm Movements." *Proceedings of the Royal Society B: Biological Sciences* 281.1794 (2014): 20141139.

4. FEELING SQUEEZED

Hertenstein, Matthew J., et al. "The Communication of Emotion via Touch." *Emotion* 9.4 (2009): 566.

Hertenstein, Matthew J., et al. "Touch Communicates Distinct Emotions." *Emotion* 6.3 (2006): 528.

5. TIME WEALTHINESS

Lang, Frieder R., and Laura L. Carstensen. "Time Counts: Future Time

Perspective, Goals, and Social Relationships." *Psychology and Aging* 17.1 (2002): 125.

Mogilner, Cassie, Zoë Chance, and Michael I. Norton. "Giving Time Gives You Time." *Psychological Science* 23.10 (2012): 1233–38.

6. THE MONEY REQUEST GAME

Arad, Ayala, and Rubinstein, Ariel. "The 11–20 Money Request Game: A Level-k Reasoning Study." *American Economic Review* 102.7 (2012): 3561–73.

7. CHOOSE YOUR CHOCOLATES

Tu, Yanping, Alex Shaw, and Ayelet Fishbach. "The Friendly Taking Effect: How Interpersonal Closeness Leads to Seemingly Selfish Yet Jointly Maximizing Choice." *Journal of Consumer Research* 42.5 (2015): 669–87.

8. BUYING EXPERIENCE

Carter, Travis J., and Thomas Gilovich. "The Relative Relativity of Material and Experiential Purchases." *Journal of Personality and Social Psychology* 98.1 (2010): 146.

9. A FOLD LIKE GOLD

Norton, Michael I., Daniel Mochon, and Dan Ariely. "The IKEA Effect: When Labor Leads to Love." *Journal of Consumer Psychology* 22.3 (2012): 453–60.

10. A REMOTE CHANCE

Todorov, Alexander, Amir Goren, and Yaacov Trope. "Probability as a Psychological Distance: Construal and Preferences." *Journal of Experimental Social Psychology* 43.3 (2007): 473–82.

11. DISTINCT REACTIONS

Molho, Catherine, et al. "Disgust and Anger Relate to Different Aggressive Responses to Moral Violations." *Psychological Science* (2017): 0956797617692000.

12. THE MIND'S EYE

Keogh, Rebecca, and Joel Pearson. "Mental Imagery and Visual Working Memory." *PLOS ONE* 6.12 (2011): e29221.

SIDEBAR: A BLIND MIND'S EYE

Keogh, Rebecca, and Joel Pearson. "The Blind Mind: No Sensory Imagery in Aphantasia." Working Paper, 2017.

Pearson, Joel, Colin W. G. Clifford, and Frank Tong. "The Functional Impact of Mental Imagery on Conscious Perception." *Current Biology* 18.13 (2008): 982–86.

13. THE BLAME GAME

Gray, Kurt, and Daniel M. Wegner. "To Escape Blame, Don't Be a Hero—Be a Victim." *Journal of Experimental Social Psychology* 47.2 (2011): 516–19.

14. TRIP THE SCRIPT

Danvers, Alexander F., and Michelle N. Shiota. "Going off Script: Effects of Awe on Memory for Script-Typical and -Irrelevant Narrative Detail." *Emotion* 17.6 (2017): 938.

Gallagher, Shaun, et al. *A Neurophenomenology of Awe and Wonder: Towards a Non-Reductionist Cognitive Science*. New York: Springer, 2015.

15. ON A POSITIVE NOTE

Reis, Harry T., et al. "Are You Happy for Me? How Sharing Positive Events with Others Provides Personal and Interpersonal Benefits." *Journal of Personality and Social Psychology* 99.2 (2010): 311.

16. A BENEVOLENT NUDGE

Aquino, Karl, et al. "Testing a Social-Cognitive Model of Moral Behavior: The Interactive Influence of Situations and Moral Identity Centrality." *Journal of Personality and Social Psychology* 97.1 (2009): 123.

17. MENTAL PICTURES

Pecher, Diane, et al. "Language Comprehenders Retain Implied Shape and Orientation of Objects." *Quarterly Journal of Experimental Psychology* 62.6 (2009): 1108–14.

Stanfield, Robert A., and Rolf A. Zwaan. "The Effect of Implied Orientation Derived from Verbal Context on Picture Recognition." *Psychological Science* 12.2 (2001): 153–56.

Zwaan, Rolf A., Robert A. Stanfield, and Richard H. Yaxley. "Language

Comprehenders Mentally Represent the Shapes of Objects." *Psychological Science* 13.2 (2002): 168–71.

18. MISS QUOTA

Cadsby, C. Bram, Song Fei, and Francis Tapon. "Are You Paying Your Employees to Cheat? An Experimental Investigation." *The B. E. Journal of Economic Analysis & Policy* 10.1, 2010.

19. CHUGGING CHALLENGE

Gneezy, Uri, John A. List, and George Wu. "The Uncertainty Effect: When a Risky Prospect Is Valued Less Than Its Worst Possible Outcome." *Quarterly Journal of Economics* 121.4 (2006): 1283–1309.

Shen, Luxi, Ayelet Fishbach, and Christopher K. Hsee. "The Motivating-Uncertainty Effect: Uncertainty Increases Resource Investment in the Process of Reward Pursuit." *Journal of Consumer Research* 41.5 (2014): 1301–15.

SIDEBAR: MAYBE IT'S LOVE

Whitchurch, Erin R., Timothy D. Wilson, and Daniel T. Gilbert. "'He Loves Me, He Loves Me Not…' Uncertainty Can Increase Romantic Attraction." *Psychological Science* 22.2 (2011): 172–75.

20. DISTORTED TRUTHS

Erickson, Thomas D., and Mark E. Mattson. "From Words to Meaning: A Semantic Illusion." *Journal of Verbal Learning and Verbal Behavior* 20.5 (1981): 540–51.

Reder, Lynne M., and Gail W. Kusbit. "Locus of the Moses Illusion: Imperfect Encoding, Retrieval, or Match?" *Journal of Memory and Language* 30.4 (1991): 385–406.

Song, Hyunjin, and Norbert Schwarz. "Fluency and the Detection of Misleading Questions: Low Processing Fluency Attenuates the Moses Illusion." *Social Cognition* 26.6 (2008): 791–99.

21. WORDS IN SPACE

Hoffmann, Danielle, et al. "The Impact of Mathematical Proficiency on the Number-Space Association." *PLOS ONE* 9.1 (2014): e85048.

Previtali, Paola, Maria Dolores de Hevia, and Luisa Girelli. "Placing Order in Space: the SNARC Effect in Serial Learning." *Experimental Brain Research* 201.3 (2010): 599–605.

22. TEMPTING YOUR IMPULSES

Shiv, Baba, and Alexander Fedorikhin. "Spontaneous Versus Controlled Influences of Stimulus-Based Affect on Choice Behavior." *Organizational Behavior and Human Decision Processes* 87.2 (2002): 342–70.

23. KARAOKE CHALLENGE

Brooks, Alison Wood. "Get Excited: Reappraising Pre-performance Anxiety as Excitement." *Journal of Experimental Psychology: General* 143.3 (2014): 1144.

Jamieson, Jeremy P., et al. "Turning the Knots in Your Stomach into Bows: Reappraising Arousal Improves Performance on the GRE." *Journal of Experimental Social Psychology* 46.1 (2010): 208–12.

SIDEBAR: EASIER TO ACCEPT

Troy, Allison S., et al. "Cognitive Reappraisal and Acceptance: Effects on Emotion, Physiology, and Perceived Cognitive Costs." *Emotion* 18.1 (2018): 58.

24. THE FAIRER SEX?

Andreoni, James, Eleanor Brown, and Isaac Rischall. "Charitable Giving by Married Couples: Who Decides and Why Does It Matter?" *Journal of Human Resources* 38.1 (2003): 111–33.

Andreoni, James, and Lise Vesterlund. "Which Is the Fair Sex? Gender Differences in Altruism." *Quarterly Journal of Economics* 116.1 (2001): 293–312.

SIDEBAR: TIPPING TENDENCIES

Conlin, Michael, Ted O'Donoghue, and Michael Lynn. "The Economics of Tipping: Implicit Contract, Repeated Game and Behavioral Responses." Working Paper, Cornell University, 1999.

25. THE WILL TO WANDER

Duckworth, Angela L., et al. "Grit: Perseverance and Passion for Long-Term Goals." *Journal of Personality and Social Psychology* 92.6 (2007): 1087.

Eskreis-Winkler, Lauren, et al. "The Grit Effect: Predicting Retention in the Military, the Workplace, School and Marriage." *Frontiers in Psychology* 5, 2014.

Ralph, Brandon C. W., et al. "Wandering Minds and Wavering Goals: Examining the Relation between Mind Wandering and Grit in Everyday Life and the Classroom." *Canadian Journal of Experimental Psychology* 71.2 (2017): 120.

26. RISKY BUSINESS

Filippin, Antonio, and Paolo Crosetto. "A Reconsideration of Gender Differences in Risk Attitudes." *Management Science* 62.11 (2016): 3138–60.

Holt, Charles A., and Susan Laury. "Risk Aversion and Incentive Effects." *American Economic Review* 92.5 (2002): 1644–55.

27. FUTURE DISCOUNT

Abdellaoui, Mohammed, Olivier l'Haridon, and Corina Paraschiv. "Do Couples Discount Future Consequences Less Than Individuals?" Working Paper, 2013.

28. GOOD, BAD, AND BETTER THAN OTHERS

Lavner, Justin A., Benjamin R. Karney, and Thomas N. Bradbury. "Newlyweds' Optimistic Forecasts of Their Marriage: For Better or for Worse?" *Journal of Family Psychology* 27.4 (2013): 531.

Murray, Sandra L., John G. Holmes, and Dale W. Griffin. "The Benefits of Positive Illusions: Idealization and the Construction of Satisfaction in Close Relationships." *Journal of Personality and Social Psychology* 70.1 (1996): 79.

Rusbult, Caryl E., et al. "Perceived Superiority in Close Relationships: Why It Exists and Persists." *Journal of Personality and Social Psychology* 79.4 (2000): 521.

29. HIGHS AND LOWS

Fujita, Kentaro, et al. "Construal Levels and Self-Control." *Journal of Personality and Social Psychology* 90.3 (2006): 351.

30. TABOO MEMORY AID

Jay, Timothy, Catherine Caldwell-Harris, and Krista King. "Recalling

Taboo and Nontaboo Words." *American Journal of Psychology* (2008): 83–103.

31. JOTTING THANKS

Toepfer, Steven M., Kelly Cichy, and Patti Peters. "Letters of Gratitude: Further Evidence for Author Benefits." *Journal of Happiness Studies* 13.1 (2012): 187–201.

SIDEBAR: GRATEFUL, AND FEELING GREAT

Bartlett, Monica Y., et al. "Gratitude: Prompting Behaviours That Build Relationships." *Cognition & Emotion* 26.1 (2012): 2–13.

Lambert, Nathaniel M., et al. "A Changed Perspective: How Gratitude Can Affect Sense of Coherence through Positive Reframing." *Journal of Positive Psychology* 4.6 (2009): 461–70.

Lambert, Nathaniel M., et al. "Benefits of Expressing Gratitude: Expressing Gratitude to a Partner Changes One's View of the Relationship." *Psychological Science* 21.4 (2010): 574–80.

32. MALLEABLE ME

Breines, Juliana G., and Serena Chen. "Self-Compassion Increases Self-Improvement Motivation." *Personality and Social Psychology Bulletin* 38.9 (2012): 1133–43.

33. MIND-MELD MEMORIES

Gabbert, Fiona, Amina Memon, and Daniel B. Wright. "Memory Conformity: Disentangling the Steps toward Influence during a Discussion." *Psychonomic Bulletin & Review* 13.3 (2006): 480–85.

Harris, Celia B., et al. "Couples as Socially Distributed Cognitive Systems: Remembering in Everyday Social and Material Contexts." *Memory Studies* 7.3 (2014): 285–97.

Vredeveldt, Annelies, Alieke Hildebrandt, and Peter J. van Koppen. "Acknowledge, Repeat, Rephrase, Elaborate: Witnesses Can Help Each Other Remember More." *Memory* 24.5 (2016): 669–82.

34. THE POWER OF US

Chen, Serena, Annette Y. Lee-Chai, and John A. Bargh. "Relationship Orientation as a Moderator of the Effects of Social Power." *Journal of Personality and Social Psychology* 80.2 (2001): 173.

Gordon, Amie M., and Serena Chen. "Does Power Help or Hurt? The Moderating Role of Self–Other Focus on Power and Perspective-Taking in Romantic Relationships." *Personality and Social Psychology Bulletin* 39.8 (2013): 1097–1110.

35. WHAT MIGHT HAVE BEEN

Kray, Laura J., et al. "From What Might Have Been to What Must Have Been: Counterfactual Thinking Creates Meaning." *Journal of Personality and Social Psychology* 98.1 (2010): 106.

36. AW, I'M TOUCHED

Debrot, Anik, et al. "Touch as an Interpersonal Emotion Regulation Process in Couples' Daily Lives: The Mediating Role of Psychological Intimacy." *Personality and Social Psychology Bulletin* 39.10 (2013): 1373–85.

Ditzen, Beate, et al. "Effects of Different Kinds of Couple Interaction on Cortisol and Heart Rate Responses to Stress in Women." *Psychoneuroendocrinology* 32.5 (2007): 565–74.

Holt-Lunstad, Julianne, Wendy A. Birmingham, and Kathleen C. Light. "Influence of a 'Warm Touch' Support Enhancement Intervention among Married Couples on Ambulatory Blood Pressure, Oxytocin, Alpha Amylase, and Cortisol." *Psychosomatic Medicine* 70.9 (2008): 976–85.

37. NOTICEABLE SUPPORT

Bolger, Niall, Adam Zuckerman, and Ronald C. Kessler. "Invisible Support and Adjustment to Stress." *Journal of Personality and Social Psychology* 79.6 (2000): 953–61.

Maisel, Natalya C., and Shelly L. Gable. "The Paradox of Received Social Support: The Importance of Responsiveness." *Psychological Science* 20.8 (2009): 928–32.

38. TRAVEL TIME

Diamond, Lisa M., Angela M. Hicks, and Kimberly D. Otter-Henderson. "Every Time You Go Away: Changes in Affect, Behavior, and Physiology Associated with Travel-Related Separations from Romantic Partners." *Journal of Personality and Social Psychology* 95.2 (2008): 385.

Niessen, Cornelia, et al. "The Impact of Preventive Coping on Business Travelers' Work and Private Life." *Journal of Organizational Behavior*. 2017.

39. CONFLICTS AND CUDDLING

Gulledge, Andrew K., Michelle H. Gulledge, and Robert F. Stahmann. "Romantic Physical Affection Types and Relationship Satisfaction." *American Journal of Family Therapy* 31.4 (2003): 233–42.

Van Raalte, Lisa J. *The Influence of Cuddling on Relational Health for Cohabiting Couples*. Arizona State University, 2017.

SIDEBAR: A KISS BEFORE PARTING

National Sleep Foundation. *2013 International Bedroom Poll*. Arlington, VA: National Sleep Foundation, 2013.

40. A MATTER OF TIME

Matlock, Teenie, Michael Ramscar, and Lera Boroditsky. "On the Experiential Link between Spatial and Temporal Language." *Cognitive Science* 29.4 (2005): 655–64.

41. MUSIC STYLE STEREOTYPES

North, Adrian C., and David J. Hargreaves. "Lifestyle Correlates of Musical Preference: 1. Relationships, Living Arrangements, Beliefs, and Crime." *Psychology of Music* 35.1 (2007): 58–87.

42. AUDIO ANALGESICS

Knox, Don, et al. "Acoustic Analysis and Mood Classification of Pain-Relieving Music." *Journal of the Acoustical Society of America* 130.3 (2011): 1673–82.

Mitchell, Laura A., Raymond A. R. MacDonald, and Eric E. Brodie. "A Comparison of the Effects of Preferred Music, Arithmetic and Humour on Cold Pressor Pain." *European Journal of Pain* 10.4 (2006): 343.

Stephens, Richard, John Atkins, and Andrew Kingston. "Swearing as a Response to Pain." *Neuroreport* 20.12 (2009): 1056–60.

43. BLIND CHOICE

Brehm, J. W. "Post-Decision Changes in the Desirability of Choice

Alternatives." *Journal of Abnormal and Social Psychology* 52 (1956): 384–89.

Chen, M. Keith, and Jane L. Risen. "Is Choice a Reliable Predictor of Choice? A Comment on Sagarin and Skowronski." *Journal of Experimental Social Psychology* 45.2 (2009): 425–27.

Sharot, Tali, Cristina M. Velasquez, and Raymond J. Dolan. "Do Decisions Shape Preference? Evidence from Blind Choice." *Psychological Science* 21.9 (2010): 1231–35.

44. MUNCH MANIPULATION

Chapman, Colin D., et al. "Watching TV and Food Intake: The Role of Content." *PLOS ONE* 9.7 (2014): e100602.

Rolls, Barbara J., Ingrid C. Fedoroff, and Joanne F. Guthrie. "Gender Differences in Eating Behavior and Body Weight Regulation." *Health Psychology* 10.2 (1991): 133.

SIDEBAR: GENDERED MEAL PREFERENCES

Cavazza, Nicoletta, Margherita Guidetti, and Fabrizio Butera. "The Gender-Based Stereotype about Food Is on the Table. Food Choice Also Depends on Co-eater's Gender." *Psicologia Sociale* 10.2 (2015): 161-172.

45. HUMOR ME

Cann, Arnie, Heather B. Davis, and Christine L. Zapata. "Humor Styles and Relationship Satisfaction in Dating Couples: Perceived versus Self-Reported Humor Styles as Predictors of Satisfaction." *Humor: International Journal of Humor Research* 24.1 (2011): 1.

Cann, Arnie, and Katherine C. Etzel. "Remembering and Anticipating Stressors: Positive Personality Mediates the Relationship with Sense of Humor." *Humor: International Journal of Humor Research* (2008): 157–78.

SIDEBAR: COMIC, OR SANS?

Bressler, Eric R., Rod A. Martin, and Sigal Balshine. "Production and Appreciation of Humor as Sexually Selected Traits." *Evolution and Human Behavior* 27.2 (2006): 121–30.

46. SUCH A TEASE

Kruger, Justin, Cameron L. Gordon, and Jeff Kuban. "Intentions in Teasing: When 'Just Kidding' Just Isn't Good Enough." *Journal of Personality and Social Psychology* 90.3 (2006): 412.

47. SODA STICKER SHOCK

Caruso, Eugene M. "When the Future Feels Worse than the Past: A Temporal Inconsistency in Moral Judgment." *Journal of Experimental Psychology: General* 139.4 (2010): 610.

48. EXCUSES, EXCUSES

Chesterton, G. K. *Illustrated London News*, 23 Oct. 1909.

Turri, John, and Peter Blouw. "Excuse Validation: A Study in Rule-Breaking." *Philosophical Studies* 172.3 (2015): 615–34.

49. PARENTAL PEEVES

Birditt, Kira S., et al. "Tensions in the Parent and Adult Child Relationship: Links to Solidarity and Ambivalence." *Psychology and Aging* 24.2 (2009): 287.

Birditt, Kira S., Leslie M. Rott, and Karen L. Fingerman. "'If You Can't Say Something Nice, Don't Say Anything at All': Coping with Interpersonal Tensions in the Parent-Child Relationship During Adulthood." *Journal of Family Psychology* 23.6 (2009): 769.

SIDEBAR: POLL YOUR PARENTS

Steinberg, Laurence. "We Know Some Things: Parent-Adolescent Relationships in Retrospect and Prospect." *Journal of Research on Adolescence* 11.1 (2001): 1–19.

50. THERMO-COUPLING

Hong, Jiewen, and Yacheng Sun. "Warm It Up with Love: The Effect of Physical Coldness on Liking of Romance Movies." *Journal of Consumer Research* 39.2 (2011): 293–306.

ACKNOWLEDGMENTS

ON NOVEMBER 10, 2007, I made the best decision of my life: I married Tanya. Without her backing, I could never have taken on this project, and without her love, I wouldn't have been qualified to write it. I hope we have many more years of experimenting ahead of us!

I'd also like to thank my children for their enthusiasm and encouragement during the writing process. They are the reason why I do what I do, and why it takes as long as it does.

Others who helped bring this book to life, and to whom I extend my deep gratitude, include my editor Anna Michels, my research assistant Ken Chang, and my agent Laurie Abkemeier.

ABOUT THE AUTHOR

SHAUN GALLAGHER IS THE AUTHOR of *Experimenting With Babies: 50 Amazing Science Projects You Can Perform on Your Kid* and *Correlated: Surprising Connections Between Seemingly Unrelated Things*. A former magazine and newspaper editor, he now writes books and software. He lives with his wife and children in northern Delaware.

Visit his websites:

Newlywed.science for relationship research with a focus on newlyweds.

ExperimentingWithBabies.com for news and tidbits about child-development research.

Correlated.org for crazy crowdsourced correlations and statistics.